GW00601972

Two Minutes to the Station

The Tale of Hitchin's Victorian Triangle

By Valerie Taplin and Audrey Stewart

A Hitchin Historical Society Publication

A Hitchin Historical Society Publication 2010
www.hitchinhistoricals.org.uk

© Hitchin Historical Society, Valerie Taplin and Audrey Stewart

ISBN: 978-0-9552411-5-4

Design, layout and photo-enhancing: Barrie Dack and Associates 01462 834640
Printed by: Olive Press, Stotfold, Hitchin, Herts, 01462 733333

All rights reserved. Without limiting the rights under copyright reserved
above, no part of this publication may be reproduced, stored or introduced
into a retrieval system, or transmitted, in any form or by any means (electronic,
mechanical, photocopying, recording or otherwise) without the prior written
permission of both the copyright owner and the publisher of this book.

Cover illustration: A postcard of Walsworth Road in the late 19th,
early 20th Century

Inside front cover: Hitchin Street Map 2010 (courtesy of
G.I. Barnett & Sons Ltd)

Half title page: Barley- twist chimney pots on the roof of
110 Walsworth Road

Frontispiece: Early 20th Century postcard view of Walsworth Road,
with letterhead of J.R. Gamble visible on the right
at number 32

Inside rear cover: Ordnance Survey map of Hitchin 1851
(Hitchin Museum)

Rear cover: Triangle Residents' Association sketch map used on
posters advertising meetings. Valerie Taplin and Audrey
Stewart during the last months of writing

Two Minutes to the Station

Walsworth Road, Hitchin.

Children enjoying the freedom of an empty Walsworth Road in an early 20th Century postcard J.R.Gamble (left) occupies the site of the present "Khushma Cottage" Indian Restaurant and Take-Away. The entrance to Radcliffe Road is on the left.

32 WALSWORTH ROAD,

Hitchin, ... 19 ......

....

Dr to Mrs. J. R. Gamble,

Coal, Corn, Flour Merchant, and Confectioner.

HAY, STRAW & CHAFF.

DOG BISCUITS, BIRD SEEDS, POULTRY FOODS, &c., &c.

COAL AND COKE BY TRUCK LOADS TO ANY STATION.

CONTENTS

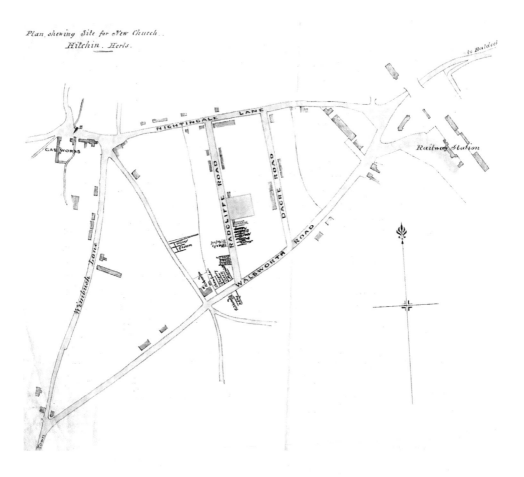

Sketch by George Beaver, Surveyor, showing the site for the Church of the Holy Saviour, circa 1863-1864
The detail on the map reveals buildings already in existence with named occupants. In Verulam Road (then called Green Lane) are Oliver and Groom. The L-shaped building in blue on the corner of Walsworth Road has the name W. Richardson. Next to that in Walsworth Road are Chamberlain, Gregory, Clark and Marriott. On the opposite side of Walsworth Road are Redhead and Adey. On the left side of Radcliffe Road, are Norris, Minnis? and Beeton? Further from the corner are Banks and Russell. On the opposite side, before the church, marked in pink, are Marsh?, Button, Armstrong, Buckle and Molly? And on the other side of the church site is Watson. (Vicar and Churchwardens of Holy Saviour Church)

Acknowledgements

This book, like so many on Hitchin's history would not have been possible without the invaluable resources of Hitchin Museum, Hitchin Library and Hertfordshire Archives and Local Studies.

In addition, we are most grateful to the following who have been very generous in providing help and information, for lending photographs and documents and for contributing memories.

Martin & Gwen Allen, Louisa Ashbee, Desmond Aves, Lesley Bacon, Berry House Veterinary Practice, Gerald Billingham, Jean Boothby, Guy Bowman, Rory Bowman, Mary Bradbeer, Stephen Bradford-Best, Mrs. Millie Bradshaw, Lionel Braybrooke, David & Vicki Brooker, Renate & Jeremy Burrowes, Wendy Cant, Cheryl Catling, Joanna Cooper, Elizabeth Cranfield, Michael Cranfield, David & Sheila Daw, Elizabeth Dew, Denis Dolan, Cilla Dyson, Audrey Eastham, Jane Eddy, Mary Else, Richard Field, Audrey Foster, the Reverend Jane Fox, Pat Gadd Thurstance, Nicholas & Jane Gainsford, Margaret Gibbs, Clarence Griffiths, Mr Haddow, Peter Hankin, Janet Hicks, Jill Higginson, Holy Saviour Church Vicar and Churchwardens, Ed & Nell Howes, Jean Hunt, David Jones, John Keene, Terry Knight, Brian Limbrick, John Lucas, Jo & Giles Maddex, Daphne Mardell, Nancy Mattausch, Amanda & Chris Maylin, Pansy Mitchell, Patsy Myatt, Peter Myatt, Bill Palmer, Rosemary Pearce, Frank Perry, Sucha Phgura, the late Margaret Richmond (who sadly died on 9th May 2010 before seeing her photographs and memories in print), Peter Rollason, Pauline Rowland, Stuart Sanders, Jenny and David Shirley, Jill Spooner, Don Studman, Barbara Swain, Mary Swain, Greta Underwood, Olive Vanklaveren, Ashley Walker, Simon Walker, Mrs Ann Wheeler, Derek Wheeler and Peter Willmott.

The following have contributed written pieces which are mostly attributed where they appear in the chapters.

Judi Billing, Bill and Wendy Bowker, Ellie Clarke, Susan Dye, Nicholas and Jane Gainsford, Simon Gainsford

Bill and Margaret Harmer, Pauline Humphries, Phil Rowe, who also gave invaluable IT help, Vicky Wyer and Richard Whitmore.

Our original artists whose drawings, many specially commissioned, appear in the book are the late Reverend Patrick Bright, Caroline Frith, Daphne Gibson, David McKeeman, Patsy Myatt and Carola Scupham.

Ellie Clarke & Derek Wheeler gallantly and swiftly proof-read the text at short notice.

We are indebted to Barrie Dack for his good-humoured guidance and for turning our text and pictures into an attractive and professional book.

Finally, but by no means least, we should never have reached publication without the experience and tremendous help and encouragement of Scilla Douglas and Pauline Humphries.

Valerie Taplin and Audrey Stewart 2010

Foreword

We were intrigued when we first heard that a book was being written about an area of Hitchin that has figured so strongly in the life of our family for several generations. We feel privileged to have been involved in some of the research and delighted with some of the previously unknown information and photographs that have been discovered along the way.

Although none of the Gainsford family currently live within the Triangle, our family ties remain strongly linked to Hitchin which has such a rich history and retains many fine ancient buildings with stories to tell. Having spent much of our childhood within the area we probably never gave much thought to the "Triangle" itself or the events that formed and influenced it. So this book has stimulated our interest and opened our eyes to many aspects of our family history, including the part they played in the history and development of this unique area.

We really hope that many will read this book and experience the same increased interest as we did.

Simon and Nicholas Gainsford

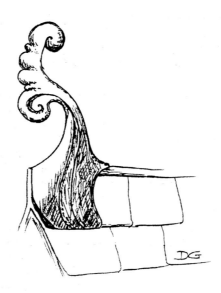

Terracotta ridge tile finial still visible on the roof of the Studman & Morgan building in Nightingale Road

From fields to early days

An Introduction

In Hitchin's historic past, its residents would have defined their Triangle as the space enclosed by what is now Queen Street and Bridge Street at the foot of Hitchin Hill. Today, however, people identify the name Triangle with quite a different part of the town. To the present day population, it means the vibrant and much newer area contained by Walsworth Road, Nightingale Road and Verulam Road, together with their "offshoots"

In 2003, Valerie Taplin of Dacre Road and Susan Dye of Walsworth Road started meeting with others to talk about the history of the Triangle and soon after began the research which has resulted in this book, mostly using the resources of Hitchin Museum and Library. The Hitchin Historical Society became involved in an advisory and encouraging capacity and various members of the HHS Committee have attended the meetings of this history group which still continues, meeting at Molly Malone's public house in Nightingale Road. Susan Dye continued for about 3 years after which Valerie Taplin carried on alone with the research.

Audrey Stewart, while churchwarden at Holy Saviour Church in the 1970s, had started sifting through the Church's documents and those held at Hitchin Museum in order to record something of the Church's history together with the associated buildings in Radcliffe Road. This was not completed, but in 2007, following her retirement, she and Valerie were introduced and it seemed sensible to share their findings. The HHS agreed to publish a book and so this work came into being.

The area was not known as The Triangle until the 1970s and 1980s. Peter Myatt, writing in the Triangle Newsletter of May 2004 explains how it came about.

Susan Dye and Valerie Taplin, front left and right, share their research results with Scilla Douglas & Pauline Humphries, back left and right in February 2004. And so it all began!

"In the winter of 1980/81 two Dacre Road residents dreamt up the idea of some kind of street festival in Dacre Road, Radcliffe Road, Nightingale Road and Ransom's Rec…

There was a strong feeling that there was a unique and vibrant community and culture in our corner of Hitchin and we wanted to celebrate this and share it. The area had developed a strong community spirit and united with some success in opposition to the council's plans to demolish large swathes in the early '70s; it was at this time that we became known as the Triangle and there was a strong sense of defiance – despite being told by our council that our houses were "not fit for pigs to live in" we were still here and proud of it!"

The demolition stopped, but not before some of the Victorian cottages had gone from Radcliffe Road and Dacre Road. The remaining cottages were updated instead with bathrooms and more modern amenities. The community spirit engendered by this turn of events has continued as is illustrated later in the book.

The first Triangle Festival took place on 25th July 1981 and the event continued for some years. Maybe it will be revived some day?

Hitchin in the mid 19th Century was the administrative, legal, commercial and banking centre of the district now known as North Hertfordshire. With the coming of the railway in 1850, the owners of land on the north eastern outskirts of the town towards the new railway station saw the possibilities of selling plots for development, a practice familiar to us today. The going rate was some £70 per acre, a princely sum at the time. The railway not only brought in many workers of its own, but it also facilitated the growth and mobility of other businesses and industries. At the end of the 19th Century and up to the middle of the 20th, this area was almost self-sufficient with all necessary shops, businesses and industries, places of worship, two schools and private teachers as well as the inevitable public houses. An interesting fact that has emerged during the research for and writing of this book is how many women in the 19th Century managed their own businesses, public houses included.

The architecture that remains of the period is typical of the Victorians, some very fine individual houses and the rest middle-class villas and terraced cottages, the latter largely for the work force on the railway. Of the three main roads, Verulam Road was and is the leafy and genteel residential area, Walsworth Road a mixture of middle class houses and some prestigious businesses and Nightingale Road the location of many small businesses.

The history of the Triangle is the history of a community, with some influential individuals and many ordinary ones, all of whom have a story to tell and we are fortunate in having a wealth of memories from long-standing residents on their life, childhood, education, work and worship in the Triangle. This book is by no means the end of the story, however, as there are still places, people and memories to discover, so the authors are continuing their research.

Particular significance is given to the Gainsford family, as they had a lasting influence on so many aspects of town life. Particular individuals are introduced in the road or building where they belonged.

Sadly the area has lost some fine Victorian and Edwardian buildings, but much has survived and is being cared for, the community is still vibrant today and the population even more varied and we have given the final word in the book to them.

Chapter  1

Impact of steam

At one apex of the Triangle lies a feature of Hitchin life that has been an essential part of the town for 160 years. The railway station was opened, along with the main line from London to York, in 1850. The disruption caused when the wide cutting was dug through the chalk to create the trackbed and station site can only be imagined. Eliza Sharples, a sixteen year old Quaker, growing up in Hitchin at the time, records the following in her diary, 26th August 1847.

"In the evening, I went for a walk by moonlight to the Railway. There are some lines laid down a very little way on which are two waggons, so we got into one of these waggons and had a short ride, for the sake of saying we had had a ride on the Great Northern Railway."

But in any event, the effect of the new means of transport on the population of Hitchin was dramatic. The thirty-two mile journey to or from London was suddenly something that could be achieved on the Great Northern Railway in a fraction of the time previously taken by a coach on the poor road network of the day, and in considerably more comfort!

The effect on the Triangle area was particularly marked, because the railway skirted the town to the east, and the station was actually nearer to Walsworth than to the centre of Hitchin. The property boom that followed, along Nightingale Road and Walsworth Road, as well as the in-fill of Dacre and Radcliffe Roads provided new housing, much of which accommodated those workers employed in the fledgling railway industry. The Great Northern, and later, in 1857, the Midland, also provided some residential accommodation for its own staff at Great Northern Cottages and Midland Cottages.

Entrance to the present Station Office on the 'down'(northbound platform). This part of the buildings dates from the 1910 re-building of the station

The passenger station was substantial from the start, with a considerable number of staff. Little remains of the structure of the original station, the only visible part being that now occupied by the coffee shop at the north end of the 'up' (southbound) platform. The distinctive semi-circular tops to the windows are clearly different from those of the rest of the station, rebuilt in 1910.

As with most railways built during this period of rapid expansion of the network, the line carried a mix of passenger and freight traffic. The Great Northern's freight operation was based mainly to the north of Nightingale Road, though sidings existed also on the site of the current car park, including those for the loading and unloading of livestock adjacent to what is now the taxi and bus turnaround, outside the front of the station buildings.

Hitchin had also the important additional role as a location for an engine shed. In the early days of railways, steam locomotives required frequent stops for taking on water, and changes of engine took place at various points along the route. As well as the taking on of water and coal, light maintenance of locos took place here.

The simple layout of a through station on a single main line did not last for long. Within months, a branch had been constructed from Hitchin to another important market town, Royston. This was extended over the following two years to Cambridge though, for some time, a through service was not provided, passengers having to change at Shepreth from the Great Northern to the Eastern Counties railway to reach the university city. Through services to and from Cambridge had to wait until 1866. All too often, in the early days of Britain's railways, political battles between rival companies engendered operating practices that resulted in the maximum inconvenience for passengers!

In 1857 the final piece in Hitchin's railway jigsaw was slotted into place with the coming of the Midland Railway to the town. The Midland had been an enterprise mainly confined to the East Midlands of England, centred on Derby, and had no route of its own to London. Until 1857, its London traffic followed a tortuous (and expensive) route from Leicester via Rugby and the London & North Western Railway to Euston. In that year it opened a more direct route from Leicester through Bedford to Hitchin, joining the Great Northern there for the final thirty-mile dash to its London markets. At the same time, the Midland opened its own freight depot in Hitchin, to the west of the Great Northern's on Nightingale Road. The weighbridge and associated office building still stands in what is now the railway engineering yard on the site.

For eleven years, Hitchin was an important junction serving three main lines from King's Cross: to Peterborough, York and beyond; to Royston, Cambridge and East Anglia; and to Bedford, Leicester and the East Midlands. In 1868, the Midland Railway – having become as irritated with the Great Northern at Hitchin as it had earlier been with the North Western at Rugby – finally completed its own route to London with the opening of the line from Bedford, through Luton and St Albans, to the new St Pancras station. The line between Bedford and Hitchin became a minor branch line overnight, a status it clung to precariously until closure to passengers at the end of 1961, freight traffic surviving only until 1964.

Nineteenth and early twentieth century census returns from the Triangle area show a wide variety of railway occupations, from signalman to driver; from clerk to fitter, and many others. No doubt, as was always the case in towns with

Station staff in 1903 with the cabbies' hut behind them, a picture taken by Hitchin photographer, T.B. Latchmore. The hut was saved by John Myatt and stood in his garden at St Bridget's in Radcliffe Road for a number of years. It was subsequently rescued by Hitchin Historical Society and restored through community effort and now stands in Hitchin Market Place. (The Fell Family)

more than one railway company, there would have been friendly but fierce rivalry between the employees of the Great Northern and the Midland. Railway servants were generally very loyal to their own company, even though their strong trades union tradition often brought them into conflict with their employer, resulting in industrial action, something which reached a peak in the General Strike of 1926, and occasionally affects services today.

Passenger train services have changed considerably over the many decades since the 1850s. We now take for granted the (usual) efficiency of a regular-interval, fast and frequent electric train service to and from London, Cambridge and Peterborough, generally with convenient connections to other destinations beyond those directly-served places. This was certainly not always the case in earlier times, and careful planning was required by the intrepid traveller of yesteryear. The passenger service in the early years of the railway was very sparse in comparison with what we have come to expect on a main line railway today. There were sometimes long gaps in the service; even as late as the early 1960s gaps of two hours or more existed between trains for destinations such as Huntingdon.

Commuting for the common man (let alone the common woman) was something that would not take place for some decades. But journey opportunities were remarkably diverse. For anyone wanting to travel outside the local area, the train was really the only option. The main line service, though not frequent, was really quite fast: a non-stop train between Hitchin and King's Cross took under an hour even in the 1860's, though a stopping train could take well over an hour.

Hitchin remained an important stop on the east coast main line to the north until the 1960s. With the development of what had been the considerably smaller town of Stevenage at this time, and finally the re-siting and rebuilding of Stevenage station in 1973, Hitchin lost its place as a stopping point for express trains, the

HITCHIN, BALDOCK, ROYSTON, SHEPRETH, and CAMBRIDGE.—Great Northern.

Fares from London			Down.	1,2,3	1&2	1,2,3	1&2	1,2,3	1&2	1&2	SUNDAYS	1,2,3	1,2,3
1 cl.	2 cl.	3 cl.	King's Cross Sta., LONDON...dep	mrn	mrn	mrn	mrn	aft	aft	aft		mrn	aft
			LONDON...dep	7e40	9 0	1027	12 0	3e50	5 0	3 15		7 30	6 0
6 0	4 6	2 8	Hitchin Junc. .dep	8 38	9 50	1140	1250	5 19	5 50	9 30		9 5	7 33
7 0	5 3	3 1	Baldock	8 47	....	1151	....	5 29	5 59	9 39		9 16	7 44
8 0	6 0	3 5½	Ashwell	8 57	....	12 1	....	5 39	....	a		9 26	7 55
8 6	6 6	3 9½	Royston	9 7	1010	1211	1 10	5 49	6 14	9 57		9 36	8 4
9 6	7 6	3 0½	Meldreth	9 14	....	1218	....	5 56	....	a		9 43	8 11
10 0	8 0	4 2½	Shepreth	9 21	....	1224	....	6 2	....	a		9 49	8 17
10 4	8 3	4 3½	Foxton	9 25	....	1228	....	6 6	....	....		9 53	8 21
10 10	8 6	4 5½	Harston	9 32	....	1233	....	6 11	c	a		9 58	8 26
11 0	8 9	4 9½	Cambridge	9 45	1030	1245	1 30	6 23	6 35	1025		1010	8 38

Up.	1,2,3	1&2	1&2	1&2	1&2	3 cl.	1,2,3	1&2	SUNDAYS	1,2,3	1,2,3
	d	b	mrn	b	aft	aft	aft	b		mrn	aft
Cambrdg (Hill's Rd)	6 40	8 5	1010	2 2	4 0		6 30	7 20		6 55	5 30
Harston	6 53	8 17	....	2 12	....		6 42	....		7 7	5 42
Foxton	6 58	8 22	....	2 17	....	Wed. only.	6 47	....		7 12	5 47
Shepreth	7 3	8 26	....	2 21	....		6 51	....		7 16	5 51
Meldreth	7 10	8 33	....	2 27	....		6 57	....		7 22	5 57
Royston	7 19	8 38	1035	2 35	4 20	5 5	7 5	7 41		7 30	6 5
Ashwell	7 29	8 47	....	2 45	....	5 20	7 15	....		7 40	6 15
Baldock	7 39	8 57	1049	2 54	....	5 45	7 24	7 55		7 49	6 24
Hitchin Junc. arr	7 50	9 8	1059	3 3	4 38	6 10	7 35	8 5		8 0	6 35
LONDON (K.C.) arr	9 35	1040	1150	4 0	5 35		9 3	9 20		9 35	7 45

a Stop to set down from Main Line Stations, if required. b 3rd class Cambridge to London.
c Stops on Mondays to set down from London. d 3rd class from Cambridge Branch to
Stations as far as Barnet, inclusive. e 3rd class from London.

1869 timetable for the line between Cambridge and London, King's Cross

last being a very early morning train carrying passengers, post and newspapers
to Leeds in the early 1970s.

As in many towns up and down the country, the railway in Hitchin provided
an inspiration for those building and naming public houses. These are described
in detail in chapter 12.

The Triangle area as we know it today might never have developed at all, had
one railway scheme actually come to fruition. Before the Midland Railway built
its line from Bedford to St Pancras in 1868, other schemes were put forward to
achieve the same result of providing the Midland with its own route to London.
One of these was the London and Midland Junction Railway. This was a scheme
of 1861 to connect the fledgling Metropolitan Railway (opened 1863) with the
Midland at Hitchin. The route was to have passed through St Albans and Codicote
before crossing Walsworth Road and Nightingale Road, roughly between Dacre
and Radcliffe Roads. The cutting through Highbury to the south of Hitchin would
have been very deep indeed but, according to the original plans in Hertfordshire
Archives and Local Studies, no tunnel was envisaged there.

25372 Hitchin. The Station. G. N. R.

An early 20th Century postcard showing Hitchin Station before the advent of motorised taxis! The horse chestnut trees were cut down in 2000. Off the picture to the right of the trees stood the cabbies' hut.

Station Approach

Station Approach is the forecourt of the railway station which was opened in 1850. The Hitchin Handbook of 1903 describes how "The Great Northern has a first class station here". Because of the many complaints of local people and passengers, however, Hitchin Urban District Council could not agree with this sentiment and pressure was brought upon Great Northern to make improvements.

The station we see today dates from a resultant rebuilding of 1910-1911, including better booking hall facilities and replacement of the original footbridge, known locally as the Hitchin 'alps' because of its hazards, with a subway. An impressive entrance canopy was added and remained until it was demolished in 1974. Improvements are still being made today and the station approach now has a large car park, bus station and taxi rank. The station is on the register of important local buildings.

Nothing stands still, and there are plans for further expansion of railway facilities in Hitchin. Network Rail has recently announced that it plans to build a new flyover for trains to Cambridge by 2014, so they will no longer have to cross the main line on the level, something which has caused delays to northbound passengers for many years. A less-well-formed plan, but one which has been talked about for years, is the reintroduction of a direct service between Oxford and Cambridge. This would involve the building of a new north-to-east curve so that trains from Bedford, via Sandy, can travel direct towards Cambridge and *vice-versa*.

Station Terrace

Station Terrace, formerly Great Northern Cottages in Station Approach was built in 1850 by the Great Northern Railway as accommodation for railway employees and the cottages are fortunately still there today and are on the register of important local buildings.

Similar housing was built nearby at the junction of Walsworth Road and Nightingale Road. These properties were demolished, and replaced by Bowman's Mill, subsequently the site of B&Q.

In 1910-1911 a new Station Master's house, "Bytham Bank" was built at the north western end of the terrace, overlooking Station Approach. This has now been converted into four residential flats.

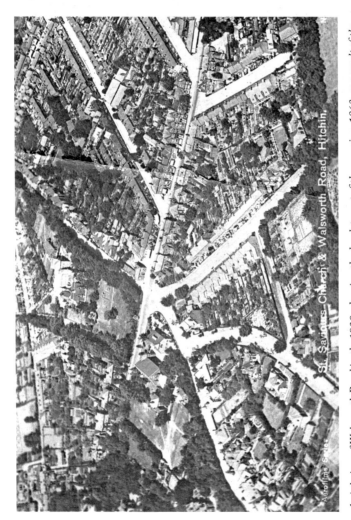

Aerial view of Walsworth Road in the 1930s showing the development of the area since 1863, as a result of the coming of the railway. Walsworth Road runs horizontally across the middle of the picture. The Sacred Heart Convent is visible on the upper left of the picture, Holy Saviour Church in the upper right and Walsworth Road Baptist Church to the left, centre. The mix of villas and rows of terraced cottages, interspersed with businesses, make up the character of the Triangle.

Chapter 2

Walsworth Road

Walsworth Road and Nightingale Road form the two long sides of the Triangle and meet at the point of the field that was known as Three Corner Field. The land was owned by William Wilshere and occupied by Henry Cannon. The 1818 plan of the town and parish of Hitchin and the map of 1844 show this as Baldock Road, leading to the hamlet of Walsworth. This road may also have been known as the Walwey. Following the opening of the railway in 1850, the stretch between Verulam Road and the station became known as Station Road and in 1889, the Local Board of Health confirmed the name as Walsworth Road.

Walsworth Road Baptist Church

Although this church is just outside the Triangle area, it is very much part of the Victorian development of the town following the arrival of the railway in 1850. As a comprehensive history has been written by Peter Hankin, this is a very brief account.

Mr Richard Johnson who from 1861 was chief engineer to the G.N.R. and a temporary member of the Tilehouse Street Baptists, owned a piece of land in Walsworth Road on which a Mission Hall was built and it opened on 9th October 1867. Congregations were so large that in 1868 a schoolroom was added with three vestries and a baptistery. In 1869, the Walsworth Road Church became a full General Baptist Church with the blessing of the Salem Chapel (Tilehouse Street).

The Hitchin builder, Mr George Jeeves, was selected to build a new church in 1873 and the foundation stone laid on 1st July 1875. Richard Johnson sold the land on which the Mission Hall stood, together with an adjacent area to the Church, and gave the Mission Hall for use as the Sunday School. The church opened with a devotional service on 23rd May 1876.

Fund-raising started in 1912 for a new Sunday School building which opened in 1915, and the old iron school building was sold to the Liberal Club in Stotfold and was still in use 70 years later..

No-one can pass the church without noticing the gardens; until around the mid-1970s, two long-serving Deacons, Mr Charlie E. Ward and Mr Cyril A. Roberts, tended the gardens voluntarily, often finishing their shifts on the railway and going directly to work on the gardens before going home. Their good work is now continued by Alan Dickinson tending the borders and Peter Hankin who cuts the grass, amongst others.

An up-to-date view of Walsworth Road Baptist Church, showing the church on the right, the hall on the left and the new ' in-fill' foyer linking the two. 2008. (Stephen Bradford-Best)

In 1992 a new enlarged vestibule was named the Richard Johnson Room after the 'founder' of the church and now in the 21st Century, there is a very modern link between the original two buildings.

Just like today, Walsworth Road has always been an important thoroughfare, linking the town to the railway station. Earlier in the Triangle's history, when people's access to goods and services was often limited to walking distance, the road was lined with an array of shops serving the daily needs of the community. It obviously drew enough local custom to support more than one baker, grocer and tailor.

A rare early 20th Century postcard of Station Road (now Walsworth Road) with horse-drawn cab on its route between town and station. The postcard was addressed to North Dakota, U.S.A. with the message "Am sending you some pc's later. Alice. Our shop is just here on the left, but you cannot see it"

Number 32 Walsworth Road as it is today. It is a fine and unusual example of vibrant, polychrome brickwork from the early 1860s. This distinctive building is now divided, but the frontage is much the same as originally built. Changing businesses reflect modern life, the recently closed tattoo parlour was replaced by an IT shop, shown here, followed by "Craft Ambrosia" for a short while. Khushma Cottage is a much favoured Indian restaurant and take-away. (Ashley Walker)

This chapter now proceeds along the left-hand side of the road towards the Railway Station, starting after the Radcliffe Arms public house which is described in Chapter 12; after the Railway Station we turn and come back along the other side of the road, finishing at the roundabout at the junction of Walsworth Road with Verulam Road .

An immaculate studio portrait of Thomas Chamberlain with his canine companion. (Hitchin Museum)

32 Walsworth Road, next to the Radcliffe Arms public house *(for more information see chapter 12)* and currently occupied by the Khushma Cottage Indian restaurant and take-away and also, recently, by "Craft Ambrosia", has seen various changes of owners and retailers from 1859 to the present date. The first occupant that we have any information on is Thomas Chamberlain

32 Walsworth Road, Thomas Chamberlain, Baker

Thomas Chamberlain was born in Hitchin in 1842 into a family living in Quaker's Alley (now West Alley). He was the second of five children and by the age of nine, the 1851 census shows that he was already contributing to the family income as a straw plaiter. His mother

9

is recorded as being a widow and a pauper. By 1861, Thomas's opportunities had increased, as he is shown as an assistant to Thomas Carling, a baker, and living in Tilehouse Street, and in 1864, he married a local girl, Eliza Swannell.

Close examination of George Beaver's map showing the planned location of St Saviour's Church in Radcliffe Road *(see frontispiece)*, shows that about this time, the Chamberlains were occupying premises next to the Radcliffe Arms in Walsworth Road. He was obviously a young man with ambition, as he established a thriving bakery business, but he also took his family responsibilities seriously. He and his wife had no children of their own, but census records show that over the decades, they made a home for a succession of nieces and nephews, and one of these at least may have been involved in the business as he is recorded as baker's assistant.

The couple later made their home in Whinbush Road where they lived to a ripe old age. Thomas died in November 1923, aged eighty two and he and Eliza are buried together in Hitchin Cemetery in St John's Road.

Although we have made the assumption that the bakery occupied the premises at 32 Walsworth Road, there is a possibility, "infilling" being a common practice in the early development of the Triangle, that it occupied the plot next door, now number 33. In 2005, Mr Jenkins, a recent owner of the premises, reported that the bakers' ovens were still 'in-situ', although now boarded up.

32 Walsworth Road, Emmanuel W. Fisher, Confectioner

Emmanuel Fisher was born in Chapman's Yard in Back Street, now Queen Street, the fifth child of Moses and Annie Fisher. His father was a scissor grinder and his mother a straw plaiter. By the time Emmanuel was 15 in 1871 he was learning a trade as a confectioner's apprentice.

During the next few years, he met his future wife, Eliza Elizabeth Dawson, known as Elizabeth, and they were married in Hitchin in 1876. In the 1881 census, Emmanuel and Elizabeth are recorded as living at 32 Station Road, now Walsworth Road, with their four children. Part of the ground floor of the building was used as a sweet shop and the rest of the house was the family's living accommodation. The warehouse where the sweets were manufactured was in Verulam Road, next to the Radcliffe Arms.

Two incidents in the history of this sweetmeat business are recorded. The first was on 3rd February 1894 when two young boys stole some sweets from Mr Fisher's warehouse in Verulam Road. According to the Hertfordshire Express reporting the Petty Sessions, Thomas Brown, aged fourteen and Walter Cook,

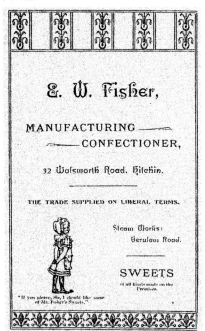

Advertisement from The Handbook to Hitchin 1899

aged twelve were the thieves. Mr E.W. Fisher, confectioner, said he missed the sweets from his warehouse on the Saturday and saw them next at the shop of Mr W.F. Morriss, the baker in Nightingale Road where it seemed they had been placed to be out of the way and not for sale. Mr Fisher had discovered that a hole had been made from the adjoining Radcliffe Arms Public House, through the wall into his warehouse and he accused Brown of making the hole.

Police Sergeant Martin had seen the sweets at Mr W.F. Morriss's shop and they were marked with blood and Brown had a cut on his hand which corresponded to a piece of bloodied glass which had been used to stop the gap in the hole in the wall. Cook also had blood on his hands as well as tar which was presumed he got from a freshly tarred fence at Mr Fisher's. Both boys' fathers vouched for their honesty and gave innocent explanations for the dirt and tar on their clothes. No sweets were found on the boys when searched at the police station and after the case had been considered by the magistrates, Mr Delmé Radcliffe as chairman dismissed the case as 'of grave suspicion, but lacking sufficient evidence'. Quite a tale of detection and witness, but the lads seemed to have been clever enough to get away with it!

Over the next few years things went well for Emmanuel and his family until in 1899, a fire broke out at the sweetmeat factory in Verulam Road. Like many people now and then, Emmanuel was not sufficiently insured for the damage caused. The Hertfordshire Express report of June 1899, describes the factory as "a detached building, with outer walls all of brick... The fire burned very fiercely owing to the combustible nature of the contents and the whole town almost was lit up by the flames. A messenger was sent for the fire brigade and the horses whose stables were nearby were got out promptly without any trouble. The captain, Mr Logsdon with his two sons and second officer Barham immediately turned out with the hose reel, leaving other members to follow with the manual engine.

It soon became apparent that the place could not be saved and the roof fell in, so their efforts were directed at preventing the flames from spreading. The crowd greatly hampered the firemen's movements, even standing on the hose which caused it to burst. Eventually, the brigade managed to attack the front of the building from a hydrant in Verulam Road; until then they had only been able to get water to the back of the building. They were further delayed by having to procure longer ladders from Mr Denniss's shop and by midday, had begun to get the fire under control, but it was some time before the crowd was dispersed.

During the night several tins of oil of peppermint exploded and some of the firemen remained on duty. The gable end next to Mr Ogden's had threatened to fall numerous times and finally collapsed on the Sunday, fortunately into the remains of the building. The chimney at the rear was pulled down as well as a portion of the other gable, where there was a landing stage from the packing room. The goods inside had been covered by the falling debris, but finally caught fire on the Sunday evening and the fire brigade had to remain until it was completely extinguished by six o'clock on the Monday morning."

The factory of three stories, built of brick had been erected only about three years previously.

"On the ground floor was the machinery for sweet making with the steam engine and boiler and about fifty bags of sugar and other raw material. There were seven or eight tons of made up goods. The second floor was used as a lozenge room which contained a large quantity of gelatine. The action of the fire upon these goods was something of the nature of a firework display and most of the firemen got several burns from the scalding sugar which spluttered about in all directions. The place was entirely burnt out and not a thing was saved, machinery, stock, building and all were destroyed and nothing but the blackened remnants of the blacker beams, the twisted iron which had formed part of the machinery and heaps of ashes remained of the sweet factory."

No cause could be ascertained for the fire and Mr Fisher was insured for only half the cost of the damage which amounted to £2,000. It was thought that the factory would be rebuilt and local opinion was that the Urban District Council should look more closely at the plans than it had done for the original building! Apparently the original plans had been only for a warehouse, not for the manufacture of sweets which caused a nuisance as no provision had been made for carrying away the fumes generated. The correspondent points out that this was a sizeable factory in the middle of a residential area.

The census records of 1901 show Emmanuel and his family still living at No 32. Sadly there are no records to show that Emmanuel rebuilt the sweet factory in Verulam Road, perhaps because he could not get planning permission. They decided to move away from Hitchin in 1902, and as we see from the following account, the sweet shop remained intact after the fire in the warehouse.

32 Walsworth Road, Thomas Brooker, Junior

Thomas Brooker, son of the founder of the Brooker's hardware business in Hitchin, married Edith Charlotte Ivory in Hitchin in 1902. They set up their first home at 32 Walsworth Road, Hitchin and took over the sweet shop that Emmanuel Fisher left behind in the same year. Before his marriage to Edith, Thomas had worked with his father in the ironmonger's shop at 48 Walsworth Road from a young age. Did he leave his wife to run the sweet shop while he continued to work for his father in the family business? By 1914 Thomas and Edith had moved to a bigger house in West Hill, Hitchin.

36, Walsworth Road, like number 32, has had many occupants. This shop on the corner of Radcliffe Road, which is now the S & K corner shop owned by the Phgura family, has mostly been a grocery business, passing from one family to another right up to the present day. It was also a Post Office; Bessie Titchmarsh, the first postmistress, combined it with her clothes shop, as detailed below. Edward Marriott was the first occupant that we know of.

36 Walsworth Road, Edward Marriott, Grocer and Accountant

Edward Marriott, his wife, Jane and their daughter Amy Lee moved to Hitchin in the early 1860's. Edward's trade was grocery, but he was also an accountant and a respected member of the community. The family lived above the shop. Edward's name appears on George Beaver's map of around 1864 *(see frontispiece)*. Evidence of his local standing is reflected in his involvement in work for the Reverend George Gainsford at St Saviour's Church. Together with a Joseph Richardson, coach builder and brother of the landlord of the "Radcliffe Arms", he audited the school, almshouses and orphanage accounts, and also witnessed important trust documents. He also housed the St Saviour' Church depot of religious literature in his shop.

E. MARRIOTT,
FAMILY GROCER & TEA DEALER,
CORNER OF
RADCLIFFE ROAD, HITCHIN.

Crosse & Blackwell's Pickles, Jams, and Marmalades,

HUNTLEY & PALMER'S BISCUITS.

BRITISH WINES!! BRITISH WINES!!

Advertisement from The Household Almanac for 1872
(Hitchin Museum?)

The 1871 census shows Edward and his family still living above the corner shop, plus two servants. Edward and Jane must have moved from Hitchin sometime before 1878 as we know from the account of Edwin George Godfrey below. In 1881 the Marriotts were living in Brixton, south London where Edward was an accountant for the tourist business.

36 Walsworth Road, Edwin George Godfrey, Grocer and Sub-Postmaster

The next grocer to occupy the premises is interesting for two reasons. He was the first to hold the position of Sub-Postmaster in the Triangle area, and secondly, because he is a good example of how a trade or profession can quickly become associated with a number of family members.

Edwin Godfrey was not "born" into the grocery business, being one of the ten children of a prosperous Shillington farmer. There were three other brothers to work the family acres, and the home was crowded, so soon after marriage, the young Mr Godfrey and his wife moved to 36 Walsworth Road, to the business vacated by the Marriott family. The Post Office opened at this address in 1878, with Edwin as its Sub-Postmaster, the first one outside the town centre, and a further indication that the St Saviour's district had achieved its own identity.

The 1881 census describes the business as a grocery, and the young Mrs Godfrey was now mother to three small children. By 1891, the family had moved to Essex, but not before they had established a network of "grocery connections". Edwin's sister, Georgina, had married William Benjamin Moss, a son of the very successful Hitchin "grocery empire", with their shop in Bancroft, warehouse in Portmill Lane, and a further store in Nightingale Road. Edwin's brother was working with a Moss family member in a Reading grocery, and another sister was married to the son of a Bucklersbury grocer. Family members would never have been short of common interests!

36 and 37 Walsworth Road, Bessie Titchmarsh, Draper and Postmistress

37 Walsworth Road stands on the corner of Radcliffe Road opposite to the S & K shop at 36 and it is now residential accommodation. Bessie Titchmarsh's long career saw her move her shop from 37 to 36 at a later date. She was to make her home at both 35 and 38 Walsworth Road.

This is an intriguing story about a young woman who probably came to live in Hitchin in the late 1880s and opened up a Ladies' and Children's underclothing, hosiery and haberdashery shop initially at 37 Station (Walsworth) Road.

Exactly why she came to live here is not known. Bessie was born in 1860 at Barrington in Cambridgeshire, one of the five children of a prosperous miller and farmer, Thomas Titchmarsh. By 1891, she had established herself in business at 37 Station Road, head of a household containing a friend, Emilie Casbolt who doubles as a "Draper's Assistant", and a domestic servant.

Ten years later, in 1901, the Titchmarsh business was still operating from No 37. Her mother, two small granddaughters and a Draper's Assistant, were now living next door at No 38 and a "friend of the family", Howard Innes Walker, described as a Brewer's Agent completed their household.

In 1908, Bessie Titchmarsh moved her drapery shop to the opposite corner of Radcliffe Road, No 36. She also expanded her operation to take on the role of postmistress at the sub-post office at the same address. And it was also "all change" for her mother's household, as she and the "family friend", Howard moved to No 35.

Howard was a widower and had been married to Louisa Christine while living in Kingsland Road, Middlesex. Louisa died sometime between 1882 and 1886. The Titchmarsh family must have thought a lot of Howard to accept him into their home. Was this why Bessie left

37 WALSWORTH ROAD, HITCHIN.

B. TITCHMARSH,

MILLINERY, ...

Ladies' & Children's Underclothing,

HOSIERY, ...

HABERDASHERY, and

General Drapery Establishment . .

* * * * * *

Specialities in INFANTS' MILLINERY.

Pelisses, Frocks, Robes, Cloaks, and every description of BABY LINEN.

Ladies' own Millinery Materials made up at moderate charges.

Agent for Mey's Celebrated WATCH-SPRING CORSETS, and Drew, Son, & Co.'s World-known Corsets, "A la Grecque."

Sole Agent for * * * * * *

P. & P. Campbell, Dyers and Cleaners, Perth.

An advertisement for Bessie Titchmarsh's shop at 37, Walsworth Road, celebrating "Infants' Millinery" and the "Mey's celebrated Watch-Spring corsets". (Handbook to Hitchin 1899)

all her personal effects and estate to Howard in her will or was there a little more to it than that? We shall never know!

In 1913, there was a fire in one of the rooms at 36 Walsworth Road.

Hitchin Fire Brigade Records, Vol. II, February 8th, 1913. "Fire at Miss Titchmarsh's shop and sub-post office, Walsworth Road, Hitchin. Discovered at 6 a.m., fire brigade not called, occupants succeeding in putting out fire themselves. Contents of one room burnt out – damage £50. Council's attention drawn to 'necessity of a system whereby the brigade may be summoned without loss of time to fires in the more distant parts of Hitchin'."

Bessie's mother, Elizabeth, died on 28th January 1914, aged 87. Probate of her will was granted to her daughter Bessie, son Arthur and Howard Walker. Over the next few years, Bessie continued to run her clothes shop and the sub-post office until late 1931 when she became ill. She moved into 35 Walsworth Road so Howard could look after her, but died on 27th January 1932, aged 72.

In February 1932, Howard sold all the stock of the late Miss Titchmarsh to C.W. Morriss, a long-established and reputable draper in the town centre.

Bessie must have been a remarkable business woman to have run a clothes shop for almost forty five years. She would have seen many changes, not only in fashion, but the coming of the motor car, and the First World War.

Howard lived on for another seven years and died on 6th February 1939, aged 87, shortly before the Second World War began.

What would make a lovely ending to this little story is to know whether there was anything more than friendship between Bessie and Howard or was it just a platonic relationship? Keeping people guessing is what makes this little gem a secret and a mystery within the Triangle.

Bessie and her mother are buried together in the same plot in the north east of the cemetery. Howard is buried in a plot to the south east of the Hitchin cemetery in St John's Road, Hitchin.

It is not known who took over the shop after Bessie died, but by 1956, Miss M. Allen was there, followed by H. Sinfield in 1959 and by the mid-1960s, it was a business called Overseas Mart.

In 1972 the shop became the S & K Superstore, named after brothers, Sucha and Karnal Phgura who had arrived in England from the Punjab in 1959 and came to King's Road, Hitchin in 1963, moving to Dacre Road in 1969. Their parents followed them a little later and the brothers both married and brought up their families here, the children all going to local schools. Like most corner shops, they are open for long hours and are patronised by regular customers and passing trade who find all the ingredients for traditional Indian cooking as well as essential groceries. The family is very community-minded and at one time Sucha's wife interpreted for her fellow countrymen at a doctor's surgery. Elderly residents in the Cloisters have been grateful to members of the staff for carrying their shopping for them. The shop and the family continue the long tradition of No 36 in serving the local residents.

37 Walsworth Road, Joseph Henry Haddow, Outfitter

An eyecatching window display fronting Mr Joseph Haddow's Outfitter's shop at 37 Walsworth Road in the early 1920s. One can only marvel at the intricate arrangement of the ranks of handkerchiefs, braces, shirts and collars and at the trustworthiness of local residents exposed to the tempting overcoats outside. Note the gas lamps! (Mr Haddow)

Joseph Henry Haddow was born to parents Charles and Elizabeth Haddow in Stevenage in 1879. Records for 1881 show them living in Albert Street, Stevenage. Joseph was only three years old when his father died, aged forty nine in 1882. In 1901, now aged twenty one, Joseph had become an outfitter's assistant and was living with his mother and sister, Elizabeth, at 61 Dacre Road, Hitchin. Joseph opened an outfitter's shop at 37 Walsworth Road, Hitchin in 1908, so he must have taken over the premises at about the time that Bessie Titchmarsh moved into No 36. He stayed there until a Mr Hubert Bangs, also an outfitter, took over the running of the shop in 1922.

37, Walsworth Road, William Arthur Leete

William Arthur Leete, also known as Les and his wife Betty, opened a grocer's shop at this address in 1958. Various occupants of the flats above the shop are listed in the local directories. The Leetes were there until 1966 when William became very ill and they had to give up the shop. Sadly he died a few months later, but Betty was a hundred years old in 2009 and still living in Hitchin, as is their daughter.

William and Betty Leete on the steps of their grocery shop, late 1950s. Mr Leete sports a pristine white coat and the couple are surrounded by "Players Please!" (Margaret Harmer)

Now, after many years of commercial use, this distinctive-looking premises is residential accommodation.

42 Walsworth Road, John Cook, Horse dealer

John Cook and his wife, Elizabeth had initially come to Hitchin in the 1860's with their nine children when his occupation was described as groom and horsekeeper. In 1871 they were living at Hill Farm in Pirton and John was known as a farmer and horse dealer, but sometime before 1881, they had moved to 42 Walsworth Road from which address he was running stables. Because of ill health, John put up the house and business for auction with George Jackson in May 1881 and died in 1882, aged 64.

His eldest son, John, continued as a horse dealer and his wife, Eliza was a dressmaker; they were living in Queen Street. John junior sadly died in 1885, aged only 42, but by 1891, his widow, Eliza had changed her occupation to wardrobe and furniture dealer.

The house and stables in Walsworth Road are still there, but the house has been altered many times, and today's appearance does not reflect the busy and noisy stable-yard that was once the life-blood of local transport.

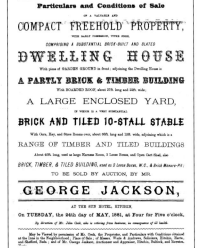

★ HORSE-DEALER'S ESTABLISHMENT. ★

WALSWORTH ROAD, HITCHIN,

On the Great Northern Railway, between the town of Hitchin and the Railway Station.

Particulars and Conditions of Sale

OF A VALUABLE AND

COMPACT FREEHOLD PROPERTY,

WITH EARLY POSSESSION, TITLES FREE,

COMPRISING A SUBSTANTIAL BRICK-BUILT AND SLATED

DWELLING HOUSE

With piece of GARDEN GROUND in front; adjoining the Dwelling House is

A PARTLY BRICK & TIMBER BUILDING

With BOARDED ROOF, about 27ft. long and 22ft. wide;

A LARGE ENCLOSED YARD,

IN WHICH IS A VERY SUBSTANTIAL

BRICK AND TILED 10-STALL STABLE

With Corn, Hay, and Store Rooms over, about 66ft. long and 15ft. wide, adjoining which is a

RANGE OF TIMBER AND TILED BUILDINGS

About 40ft. long, used as large Harness Room, 2 Loose Boxes, and Open Cart Shed, also

BRICK, TIMBER, & TILED BUILDING, used as 2 Loose Boxes, W.C., & Brick Manure-Pit;

TO BE SOLD BY AUCTION, BY MR.

GEORGE JACKSON,

AT THE SUN HOTEL, HITCHIN,

On TUESDAY, the 24th day of MAY, 1881, at Four or Five o'clock,

By direction of Mr. John Cook, who is retiring from business, in consequence of ill health.

May be Viewed by permission of Mr. Cook, the Proprietor, and Particulars with Conditions obtained at the Inns in the Neighbourhood; Place of Sale; of Messrs. Wade & Andrews, Solicitors, Hitchin, Herts., and Shefford, Beds; and of Mr. George Jackson, Auctioneer and Appraiser, Hitchin, Baldock, and Hitchin.

This comprehensive sale document details the property, unrecognisable in today's street scene. However, from the rear, evidence of the stable buildings still exists. Original sale document 1881 (Scilla Douglas)

47 Walsworth Road, The "Concrete House"

All buildings have a story to tell, but that surrounding No 47 is a particularly interesting one. It currently trades as the Driver Hire Recruitment Centre, and if you stand opposite, at the entrance to Trevor Road, even its exterior presents a very different appearance from that of its neighbours.

No 47 began life as part of a building plot, owned in 1858 by the speculative British Land Company, as did many of the houses in the road. Eventually, in 1868, this highly-desirable rectangle of "development potential" was bought by a well-known Hitchin figure, George Davis Groom.

Acacia Hotel with the Tabner family. Note the intricate concrete detail to the front wall and upper storey. (Beds & Herts Pictorial, January 1926)

His splendid new plot extended right round the corner into Dacre Road, taking in the site of the present Albert public house.

The ink was scarcely dry on the sale document before Mr Groom was busy leasing a building plot to a "William Dove Andrews (Bricklayer)", for 99 years. This stipulated that he was to build "within two years, in brick or cement block, at least 60 square yards in area and 18 feet (minimum) to rafters" a house costing at least £200, with a four foot Right of Way into Dacre Road. All this was to be completed "in a substantial and workmanlike manner".

The rear wall of No 48 in 1999 with the initials of the original owner still clearly visible from the time George Groom leased the plot of land.

Time passed. Exactly two years later, on Christmas Day, 1870, Mr Groom and Mr Andrews entered into a further agreement. More land was leased to the north and east of the plot, and the Right of Way became an eight foot Right of Carriageway into Dacre Road.

There were two interesting things about the agreements. The first is the mention of "cement block" as a possible method of construction. In 1868 this would have been highly innovative. Although natural cements had been around for millions of years, experiments leading to the patenting of artificial cements were a 19th century phenomenon, and the 1860s were at the very beginning of the era when the use of these materials would have been considered. Secondly, the choice of builder was unusual. William Dove Andrews was not a local resident (there were many reputable builders in the town) and he was a builder and plasterer. The terms "builder" and "bricklayer" were interchangeable at that time, but "plasterer" is interesting, and has a bearing on his Hitchin legacy, because William Dove Andrews constructed a concrete house.

Not only was the exterior built from cement blocks, but concrete mouldings of every description adorned both the exterior and interior. The present frontage is much modified, but traces remain in the ornate pediment. The façade, photographed ninety years ago, boasted ornamental urns, elaborate door cases and an intricate fronting wall. Internally it was a wonder to behold with moulded skirting boards, staircase and a coffin-like bath with header tank.

And who was to occupy this unusual and commodious house? A Rental Agreement of February 1873 exists between Mr W.D. Andrews and Mr A. Whittome, Bedford Road, Hitchin, a Manufacturer's Agent, for £32 per annum, with an option to buy after three years (later declined). The 1871 census shows Alfred Whittome (35), and his wife Anne (both born outside the town), and a local servant. Alfred Whittome was a Commercial Traveller in Drapery. Perhaps proximity to the Station was an attraction, although No 47, (now officially "Paragon House"), was a very commodious little dwelling. The Oxford English Dictionary defines "paragon" as "a model of excellence, or of particular quality".

Before long the Whittome family had moved on, leaving "The Paragon" (as it was now referred to) vacant. In June 1875, the Hawkins family took possession. The signatory of the new lease, "Albert Hawkins Esq.", was the third son of a well-respected local family. Albert is described in the 1871 census as "Assistant Surgeon, Royal Artillery, (Half Pay)", when he was living in Bancroft with his widowed mother, sister, and a "Domestic Nurse".

Albert Hawkins was an interesting man. As a newly qualified doctor, he had worked amongst the miners in Merthyr Tydfil, before enlisting in the Army. He endured eighteen months in the trenches during the Crimean War, before being sent with his regiment as part of an Expeditionary Force to China, where we were engaged in the Opium Wars. Subsequently, the Regiment was sent to Hong Kong, where the poor young man was "struck down by paralysis", putting an end to his career at the age of thirty. He returned home, where he lived for a further twenty years, "where no-one has ever known him complain, or exact, or expect services because of his infirmity". He became "the unconventional figure that will be seen no more in the roads and lanes about Hitchin", as a touching obituary noted in 1883. Clearly a man of courage and distinction.

"The Paragon" was to stay in the occupation of the family until 1902, Albert Hawkins buying the freehold from George Davis Groom in 1877. When his elderly mother died, his sister, Annie, continued to live there in quiet respectability, supported by a maid.

With the new century came a new identity. Station Road, as Walsworth Road was known at that time, was becoming increasingly busy, opening up the possibility of trade with passers-by. "The Paragon" was to be transformed from a domestic residence into a commercial possibility. Enter the Tabner family!

Although the 1901 census lists William Tabner (born 1869, King's Cross), as a "Fishmonger", this may well have been a temporary occupation. He had recently married into the Furr family, renowned in the area as purveyors of wet and fried fish. Together he and his wife Mary founded "The Acacias Commercial and Temperance Hotel", which, with the little dining room incorporated into the façade, was to become part of the street scene for over fifty years. Early photographs show three acacia trees behind the ornate front wall. "The Acacias" was definitely a successful little enterprise, as a Trade Directory of 1921 described, "Excellent accommodation; also dining and tea rooms, luncheons and suppers served immediately to order: cyclists and commercial gentlemen specially catered for".

However not all publicity is welcome publicity! In January 1926, the little hotel hit the national headlines with a thrilling tale of local detective-work, or as the local "Beds. and Herts. Pictorial" proclaimed , "Murder Suspect arrested at Hitchin: Hotel Keeper informs Police". And it was indeed a tale to excite the reader, although to modern eyes it seems a sad little story. A young London tailor, Eugene De Vere, who was handicapped by a wooden leg, was jilted by his seventeen-year-old girlfriend, Polly Walker. He slapped her in anger, she retaliated, and the sorry incident ended when he strangled her.

He left the scene in Camden Town and eventually walked as far as Hitchin, where he checked in at "The Acacias". What followed sounds like pure detective fiction. Mrs Tabner, an eager reader of the national press, recognised De Vere from his photograph, and the police were alerted. Police Constable Sanders arrived in plain clothes, and seating himself at a table close to the young man, "accidentally" contrived to kick his leg. On finding that it was, in truth, wooden, De Vere was arrested and charged with murder. Despite the jury's recommendation for mercy, he was executed at Pentonville Prison in March 1926, aged 27 years.

William Tabner died in 1946, and Mary, his wife, soon afterwards. Son Harold was obviously active in the business, as newspaper advertisements from the mid-1930s show that he promoted excursions from "47 Station Road", weekly seaside trips in summer, and, memorably, "a bus from the Market Square, at 10.30 a.m. onwards to where Sir Alan Cobham starts his flights". Cobham was an aviation pioneer whose "Flying Circus" toured the country visiting hundreds of sites, and giving many people their first experience of flying. In Hitchin he operated from The Meads, which were then on the outskirts of the town.

Harold and his wife, Amelia Grace Tabner, inherited the property from his mother, but they were no longer living there, but in Ickleford. In 1950, the business was sold to Ernest Arthur Hayden, who became the proprietor. Amelia Grace, Harold's widow, lived on into her nineties and in 1971 sold the property, ending a long family association. Recent years have seen new tenants, notably Mary Collins (Furniture Ltd) and Brantwood Antiques and even more modifications.

The transition of this unusual little family residence into commercial premises must have been a daunting task. Thankfully, some traces of its interesting past lie both within and without, albeit masked by partitions. Long may they remain!

48, 49, 50a, 50b and 50c Walsworth Road, T. Brooker & Sons Ltd

Thomas Brooker came to Hitchin in 1875 when he was twenty one years old, from Burstow, near Godalming in Surrey. He was from a farming background but branched out into the hardware business with his first shop in what was then Station Road, Hitchin. This was next to the present Albert public house (see Chapter 12). The property was sold to him for £178. There were still cornfields in the Dacre Road area at that time, so he was well-placed to supply local farms with agricultural implements.

A 1960s photograph of Brooker's furnishing department in Station Road. (Hitchin Museum)

He married Miss Eliza Silk in 1877. She was a draper's assistant and a close neighbour of Thomas. Thomas and Eliza produced a family of eight, the first-born in 1879, was also called Thomas. From this first family came the dynasty of the well-known business which still thrives in Hitchin today. The Herts Pictorial of 5th June 1953 states "In every household in the district is to be found something from the shops of Messrs Brooker..." and this may well hold true more than half a century later.

As the family grew, so did the business and by 1898 a branch was established at 39 Bucklersbury, now the main outlet in the town centre. Five years later, Thomas decided to start a furniture shop on the opposite corner of Dacre Road. A second storey was planned, but never came to fruition. The premises were extensive, however, as the basement was the same size as the ground floor shop and used to display furnishings of all kinds. The hardware shop had already expanded by taking over the premises next door, and by 1901, the family were living at 86 Walsworth Road

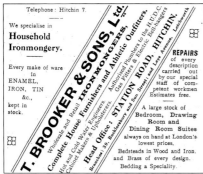

In 1904, Brooker's opened an ironmongery shop in the new Letchworth Garden City. The business continued to grow and, in 1909, became a limited company. In 1915 the firm acquired the premises of Williams & Son, furnishing ironmongers in Sun Street. The war then intervened, however, and it was 1922 before Thomas opened a furnishing department in Letchworth. Although Thomas was obviously a man of great enterprise and business acumen, he also found time for sport. He was a member of the North

Advertisement from the Hitchin Household Almanack and Directory 1926

Herts Bowling Club and became president of the newly resuscitated Hitchin Bowling Club in 1929.

Thomas finally retired from the business in 1931 and died on 13th May 1936, aged 82, his wife having died in 1908, aged 58. By the time of his death the family had added thirteen grandchildren and three great grandchildren. His eldest son, Thomas, took over as managing director, but sadly survived his father by only eleven days.

Thomas's death coming so soon after his father's was not only mourned by the family and the firm but the town too as he had been active in the community and an Urban District Councillor. The other brothers continued in the business, Harold Ernest surviving until 1953, aged seventy three, also a bowls player and the youngest, Cecil carrying on together with grandsons Tom, Arthur, Jim and Phillip. The family had occupied various houses in Walsworth Road and Harold lived at 25 Verulam Road.

Mr Tom Brooker who came to Hitchin in 1875 and opened his first shop next to the "Albert" Public House in what was then Station Road. (David Brooker)

Brooker's has been well-served by its employees over the years, some of them very long-serving. The long-term furniture shop manager, Frank Gibbs, arrived soon after the First World War, still in his army uniform! Peter Hankin lived at 72 Dacre Road for about twenty years, from the age of three in 1939. His father John worked in the furnishing shop from 1920 to 1970. When he was called up in the Second World War, Peter's mother, Emily started working there in order to keep the job open for her husband, but she stayed on when he came back and had completed thirty years when they both retired in 1970.

Not simply a piece of wood, but an historic artefact! This is now part of the mantlepiece in a Brooker household, but it began life as the counter in their shop in Walsworth Road. David Brooker remembers "When the Queen Mother was at school in Dacre Road, the governess used to bring her in and sit her on the counter while she was doing her various shopping for the family.... We have the Queen Mother's bum print!" The fascinating little brass coin-tester screwed to the edge of the counter was made by Bert and Ernie Parsell who ran the workshop. "It was used to make sure that silver coins had no pewter in them...they would appear to be alright but by putting it in that little slot and wiggling it with their thumb they could check that it was good....for your 3d piece, your 6d, your shilling, your florin, your half-crown" Pewter is much softer. (Scilla Douglas)

T Brooker & Sons Hitchin, staff photograph by Peter Hankin in 1953
Back Row: *Percy Spencer, Dick Tunnah, George Taylor, Dennis Cooper, Albert Sale, Reg Nottingham, Bob Kingsley, Stan Pearce, Bill Bell, Alf Evans, ?, Leslie Braybrooke*
Row 4: *Peter Dellar, Percy Emery, William(Wally) Lockwood, Bill Pryor, George Payne, ?, Peter Allingham, Bert Parsell, Archie Chapman, ?, John Hankin*
Row 3: *Bert Tot, Peter Worbey, Frank Hibbert, Brian Limbrick, George Holloway, Pop Richards, Ron Osbourn, Sid Roblett, ?, Jock Gilchrist, ?, Sid Springett, John Clark*
Row 2: *Florence Marfleet, Mrs Gravestock, Emily Hankin, Sheila Albone, Pauline Rush, Mrs Bett Day, Ann Pring, Miss Brown, Alice Webb, Florrie Tomlin, Winifred Fowler, Mrs Gascoyne, Mrs Mann, ?, Mildred Brooker*
Front Row: *Ken Snoad, Bob Stevens, Mr Gascoyne, Harry Jarman, Phil Brooker, Jim Brooker, Cecil Brooker, Tom Brooker, Arthur Brooker, George Walker, Frank Gibbs, Sid Lines, Frank Gravestock, Ernie Parsell*
Missing: *Bert Elson (in hospital), Bill Hogben (on holiday)*

Peter remembers thus – "My fond memories as a lad returning from St Saviour's School are going into Brooker's furnishing shop and bouncing away on the piles of carpets and on the many beds whilst waiting for my mother to finish work and walk down the road home. We lived at the top of Dacre Road then".

The hardware shop closed around 1965, some years before the furniture shop which was still trading with gas and camping sales until 1983. There is no longer a Brooker's presence in Walsworth Road. The building is now Gila Timur Trading Co. which took it over from the Mirror Palace in recent years.

The workshops in Dacre Road *(see page 80)* carried out a variety of trades: plumbing and gas fitting, metal-work and lawn-mower servicing

Photograph taken from the office over the ironmongery shop at 48 Walsworth Road. The tea is being brought from Tabner's Cafe (attached to the Acacia Hotel next door) and Day's, the Greengrocer's are receiving a delivery from A.E.Inskip, a Market Gardener from Maulden, Beds. (David Brooker)

(George Payne and the Parsell brothers). Upstairs there was an upholsterer's and a French-polishing shop, the managers of both doubling as carpet- and lino-fitters.

Long-serving employees

Ironmongery, Walsworth Road/ Dacre Road		Furnishing	
1906	George Payne	1919	Frank Gibbs, Manager, retired 1970
1920	Harry Jarman	1920	John Hankin, retired 1970
1925	George Walker	1940	Emily Hankin, retired 1970
	George Taylor		
	Mr Blows	**Furnishing Workshop**	
	Mrs Cotton		Bert Parsell
	Harold Brooker		Ernie Parsell
		1920	Alf Evans
			Archie Chapman

52 Walsworth Road, A.G. Samm amd G.W. Samm, Chemists

Samm the Chemist was a well-established presence on Walsworth Road. It was evident from the framed certificate in his shop that he had qualified as a pharmacist in 1913. Mary Else, born in 1923, and now living in Trevor Road, has fond memories of a special brew that he gave her as a child to cure her car sickness; the origins of the potion went back to the First World War. It certainly worked. Derek Wheeler lived for a short time above Frost's cycle shop and remembers that Mr Samm regularly escorted the two Misses Wilshere home from Church on Sundays to Trevor Road. He was very tall and looked as if he were buttressed by the ladies each side of him. In his shop, he peered over his spectacles at customers and Derek remembers thinking of him as something of an alchemist.

An advertisement (top)from the Hitchin Directory of 1931. Mr Samm (Tel. 152) provided a splendid service to the Triangle residents, generally working an eleven hour day and even opening on Sundays. (Right) The exterior of Mr Samm the Chemist's at No 52, probably taken in the 1950s. Note the smart unattended bicycle, left at the kerbside! (Hitchin Museum)

53 Walsworth Road, James Pepper, Monumental & General Mason

James Pepper was certainly established at 53 Walsworth Road by 1901, when the census shows him as a Sculptor and Mason aged 45, (employer), "born in Shefford".

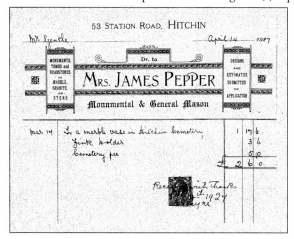

Earlier in his career he had been described as a "Stone Carver". His wife, Louisa, daughter of John Joseph Payne, obviously played a prominent role in the business. They were the only occupants at the address. By 1927, the business was owned and run by the Misses Elizabeth and Emma Payne (presumably relations of Louisa) who were still there in 1932.

59-68 Walsworth Road.

Ralph E. Sanders & Sons Ltd, Coachbuilders

The founder of this firm, Ralph Erskine Sanders was born in 1851 at Buntingford, son of a coachbuilder and the youngest of four brothers. Ralph arrived in Royston in 1875 and by 1876 had opened his own coachbuilding business. It must have thrived, as in 1898 he was able to buy Odell's coachbuilding business in Bridge Street, Hitchin and then built the extensive premises in Walsworth Road, in 1907-1908 consisting of a showroom and all the different workshops necessary for the trade. The transfer of the business from Bridge Street took place over a period of years.

After his death in 1933, aged eighty two, the company was continued by his eldest son, Ralph Francis Wilkins Sanders, known as Frank, and two of his brothers. When Frank died in 1949, it was run for a few years by his son, Bernard and Frank's brother, Royston before being sold to the Stevenage Motor Company who again sold it on and sadly it soon closed completely.

Many vehicles built by Sanders were bespoke and Ralph travelled widely to get fittings suitable for his designs, many of these fittings coming from Sweden. While they did not make vehicles on the Hitchin site, they fitted bodies to the high-class proprietary

Ralph Erskine Sanders, founder of the Royston coachbuilding firm which took over premises in Hitchin in 1898.
(Stuart Sanders)

Sanders garage in the early 1930s. The car nearest, an Austin 12 of about 1932, with a Cambridgeshire registration number, probably belonged to Lancelot Vivian Erskine Sanders, son of the founder. The family story is that he used to push the car out of his garage at 6, Wymondley Road and coast down The Avenue to the garage in Walsworth Road without switching on the engine! (Stuart Sanders).

chassis and sold them as completed vehicles. At the beginning, of course, the vehicles were horse-drawn, but the company skilfully converted to the motorised version. As well as the beautifully designed and built cars, there was a variety of other vehicles, some of which are still occasionally spotted bearing the Sanders name. One horse-drawn model could be seen for a while in London Zoo, and another appeared in a show in Surrey. A small cart even appeared as far afield as Canada some years ago.

The company was widely known, both at home and abroad and people came from afar to buy their cars.

There was even a railway truck especially for the company which not only transported their materials, but extended the advertising.

Advertisements also adorned the railway bridges on the Cambridge Road and in Little Wymondley

The buildings must have been impressive in the company's heyday. The building now housing Kwikfit was the mechanics' workshop. Sadly the beautifully arched windows and doorway on the ground floor have gone, but the arched window at the upper level on the side is still visible. The next building in the direction of the railway station was the showroom. It was also here that

Covered motor car truck advertising Sanders. (Vehicle no. 1675. 6 November 1913. Doncaster DON_9N. (National Railway Museum/Science & Society Picture Library)

films were shown before Hitchin acquired its first cinema, Blake's in Ickleford Road. Near to this was the repair bay with pits, then came the stores and finally the paint shop. The upper storey, a display area, was served by a lift with a differential gear for transporting coaches up and across to all the buildings at first floor level. There was also a carpentry shop on this level and an area next to No 58 Walsworth Road which was let out to a man who did specialist painting, Herbert Sharpe, the banner maker. The first floor was largely for storage, however.

A grandson of Ralph, Stuart Sanders, has the following to say about the company:-

"Apart from the family there were a lot of very loyal staff. I do think it is important and, sadly today very often neglected, that staff do constitute very much part of a business. And whilst we are talking 50 or 60 years ago, I remember the various people who were in charge. There was a chap named Bill Hall who was in charge of the blacksmiths' shop, Froy in the paint shop and Brown in the stores. There was Mr Bottoms and Mr Cushing who managed the mechanical side of it all. And to me they were like fixtures and fittings within the business part of it. The business just wouldn't have been the same without them and, unlike modern trades and businesses where people seem to come and go, these people were there all the time. So it's a great pity in a way that all this had to go but it has.

My early recollections of the business go back to the time of the war when it was quite difficult. The nation concentrating all its effort and personnel in the war effort, it was not very easy to run a garage and a motor business. All that time petrol was rationed, staff were hard to come by, it was quite a lean time. Nevertheless it all kept going. I remember all the iron railings being taken away by a man with an oxyacetylene torch and everything that was metal and could be used for the war effort. I don't know if it was ever used for the war effort and you can still see the stumps of these bits of metal in many of the front gardens and walls.

Soon after the war I remember seeing the business build up, the agencies got going, new cars were coming on, it took a few years, it wasn't really till the 1950s that we got the Rover and Jaguar agencies going".

Stuart Sanders also remembers that his grandfather bought the old Kershaw's Coach and stored it at the Walsworth Road premises and the original oil painting of the coach by Shayer was given by his father, Frank, to the Urban District Council in December, 1938. It now hangs in Hitchin Museum. It is not known what became of the coach itself.

Herbert Sharpe, Banner Maker

Herbert Sharpe started his career in 1906 at Tuthills Banner factory in City Road, London. This area was badly bombed during the Second World War and by 1946, Herbert had set up his own studio above Sanders garage in Walsworth Road, Hitchin. He was the man who did the special painting mentioned previously. He still kept links with his old company, but they had by this time moved to Chesham.

The Hitchin studio soon became a thriving business and was at the centre of the banner-making industry. For over twenty years the beautiful silk banners carried by trade unions all over the country were made in this studio. Sharpe's clients also included Masonic lodges and the Orange lodges of Northern Ireland, guilds and even Sunday schools. They also made other items such as sashes for beauty queens, and flags. The flag of the new Nigeria which gained its independence on 1st October 1960, was made here in Hitchin.

The production was by hand; artists used gold and aluminium leaf in working their designs

Mr Sharpe at work on a banner.

onto the silk stretched over frames. Favourite subjects for trade unions were Keir Hardie and Clement Attlee and for Orange lodges, predictably King William III (King Billy). In 1953 Herbert received a special commission from Enniskillen to produce a banner depicting the new Queen Elizabeth II to be carried in a coronation procession in Toronto, Canada.

Herbert himself was still painting in 1957, but soon after that he passed the business on to his daughter, Mrs E. Fry. Around this time, the studio moved to Tilehouse Street on a site which eventually became part of the gun shop, Barham's, also now departed. The business was bought out by Turtle and Pearce, a London company which is still making flags and hand-painted banners to this day in Borough High Street, London.

Mrs Joanna Cooper (*née* Sanders) remembers: "I used to get off the train and go down to the garage on my way home. I'd go up to the Banner Workshop to see Mr Sharpe at work. The style of art was quite unbelievable! Huge, ornate banners for mining people or Northern Irish religious ones...."Orange Men".... beautifully painted on silk, oil paint, I think, with a tiny little brush. And the smells, quite incredible, and such a contrast to the garage oil and grease. When I was teaching in Harpenden, my school, St George's, celebrated its Centenary. Mr Sharpe kindly painted a cotton flag for us – that was in 1953 or 4"

G.H. Innes & Co; Innes, Sons & King; Geo.W.King Ltd

George Harding Innes started his business on Market Hill, Royston as an agricultural

G.H. INNES & Co.,

Agricultural and General Engineers,
Iron and Brass Founders,
Agricultural Machinery Manufacturers and Merchants

INNES & Co's. PATENT HAY AND CORN STRAW
ELEVATORS,
With Fixed, Raising or Lowering Hoppers.
Thousands in use throughout the world.
The most perfect machine of its class.

INNES & Co's. PATENT PORTABLE
Chaff Cutters,
AND
Fixed Chaff Cutters and Sifters,
as used by the leading Railway Companies, Fodder Merchants, &c.

In addition to the manufacture of Specialities as above, &c., Messrs. INNES & Co. are agents for all the leading makers of
MACHINERY for all Farm and Estate Purposes.
Ploughs, Harrows, Rollers, Cultivators, Drills, Grass Mowers, Rakes, Swath Turners, Side Rakes, Binders, Reapers, Binder Twine, Oil Engines and Barn Machinery supplied and fixed. Cream Separators, Churns and Dairy Plant supplied and fixed. Farm and Contractors' Carts, Waggons, Lurries, Milk Floats, &c.
Steam Engines & Thrashing Machinery.
Our **Iron Foundry** is replete with modern appliances for turning out **Castings** for Builders and Contractors, &c.
Manufactory :   *Full Catalogue on application.*
STATION IRONWORKS, HITCHIN.
Attendance at Hitchin, Hertford, Cambridge, Bedford, Luton, and St. Albans Markets.
REPAIRS OF EVERY DESCRIPTION AT QUICK NOTICE.

Advertisement from the Hitchin Household Almanack 1915

An early postcard. On the back is written "Inns (sic) & Sons Shell Factory Walsworth Road behind Bowmans Flour Mill.". (Pansy Mitchell)

and furnishing ironmonger. He soon moved to new premises in Market Place, Hitchin. In 1898, he took his son, Augustus Montague, into the business and later father and son jointly presented their invention relating to improvements in the feed wells of chaff cutters to the Patent Office.

George Walter King had taken over the firm during the First World War and it then became Innes, Sons and King. George was an American whose real name was Henry Mayer (Dame Thea King, a member of the family was a renowned clarinet player, one of a number of young musicians inspired by Henry Wood during his sojourn in Hertfordshire during the Second World War). George increased production of agricultural implements and widened the range to include high class dairy equipment.

They eventually moved to more suitable premises which they had built in Walsworth Road near the railway station.

Later the product range expanded into conveyors and sliding doors, heavy lifting gear and mechanical handling machinery of all kinds. In 1952, the firm moved to its other site in Stevenage because of the cramped conditions.

The De Havilland Aircraft Company moved into the vacated premises during the 1950s and, by the mid-1960s, it was occupied by Hawker Siddeley Aviation Ltd (De Havilland Aircraft was acquired by Hawker Siddeley Aviation in 1959). In 1977 it became a founding component of the nationalised British Aerospace (BAe). In 1971, the building became a branch of Staples Mattresses but was demolished in the 1980s and factory units built in its place.

The Staples building in 1982 shortly before it was demolished. The two wooden gauging poles in the foreground alerted lorry drivers to the height of the railway bridge (Hitchin Museum)

Today, blocks of flats have been built where this important engineering business used to be. Recently King's business in Stevenage has also closed.

72 Walsworth Road, The Carrington Family of Tailors

The Carringtons were one of several families of Tailors who lived and worked in the Triangle and whose skills were passed from father to son, and down the generations.

Their tiny cottage stood next to Bowman's Mill and it was there that a young, married George Carrington set up business as a tailor some time before 1871. He had been born in Luton, the fourth son of a tailor, with whom he had originally worked.

George's family rapidly expanded, and by 1881, he and his wife had four sons and two daughters, one of whom was local resident Derek Wheeler's grandmother. Derek remarks that the babies slept in the drawers of a chest of drawers! George was described in the census as "Tailor and Grocer" and his eldest son, another George, was also a tailor in 1891, presumably working with his father. After his marriage in 1895, this George left the family home and went to live at 14 Benslow Lane where he was still living in 1952.

Meanwhile, back at No 72, the 1901 census records that another son, Sidney, aged 16, was also a tailor and had presumably entered the family business, which continued until the mid-1930s, bringing to an end 60 years of cutting and fitting skills passed down the generations of this family.

Bowman's Mill/Station Mill

The story of James Bowman and Sons begins at Astwick near Biggleswade in 1857. Samuel Bowman, a Stotfold farmer, bought "a newly-built brick and slate Water Corn Mill" to set up his sons in business. Soon, one son, James, bought his siblings out and with hard work and innovation - he introduced steam power to what had been a water mill – eventually needed to expand production. Proximity to the railway had opened up opportunities in London. The railway could move Bowman's flour to a warehouse in King's Cross and deliver it to city bakers.

In 1900, an opportunity arose when James' two sons were ready to enter the business. A plot of land was purchased opposite Hitchin Station and in 1901, the company built a steam-powered mill incorporating all the latest technology.

Over the years that followed, constant expansion and refinement took place on site. Early on, the sons were in charge of operations, supervised by their father who had, according to the Company history, a private telephone line from the mill direct to the Astwick H.Q! Efficiency was increased by the purchase of company steam-wagons to replace the horse and cart. Offley Hill with its steep gradient could be tackled with ease, at 12 m.p.h., puffing clouds of smoke and steam. These remained in use until the 1930s.

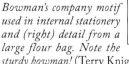

Bowman's company motif used in internal stationery and (right) detail from a large flour bag. Note the sturdy bowman! (Terry Knight)

Over the years, Station Mill encountered and overcame many difficulties, including two World Wars, the Depression and the General Strike. Strict

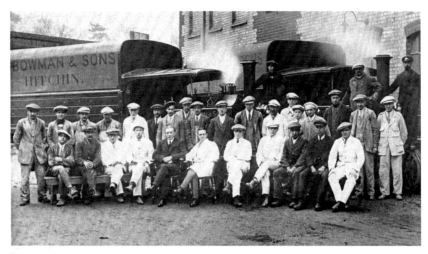

The workforce at Bowman's Mill ranged before their trusty Foden steam wagons, the mill building in the background. With the exception of the two gentlemen front centre (the Bowman brothers?), all are wearing caps. Photographed in 1922 by Hitchin photographer, F.C Sharp. *Courtesy of Terry Knight*

government regulation, conscription and the need to operate the machinery almost non-stop, meant that by 1947, there was need for serious new investment in plant and machinery. The Second World War, however, brought some benefits; two members of the Bowman family, Lizzie and Jessie, became outstanding performers in Henry Wood's orchestra. He inspired a number of young local musicians while he was living in Hertfordshire during the war. Station Mill was converted to electricity, but in August that year, an overheated bearing caused a serious fire to break out and destroy much of the wheat-storage capacity. The local "retained" (or part-time) firemen were swiftly on site, and led by a local builder who was familiar with the lay-out of the buildings, were able to save the main plant. Although the following day was a Bank Holiday, almost the entire work force turned out to begin the clear-up. Production began again within a week, although it was a year before new storage was in place.

Milling technology constantly advanced and the site was crowded. When, in 1949, a laboratory was established, it was imaginatively built as a "bridge" linking the mill with its offices. This development was important, as Bowman's could now produce more technically advanced products which were essential now that small firms were being "gobbled up" by big conglomerates. By the end of the 1960s, however, the Station Mill site was incapable of further expansion, despite the purchase and demolition of the adjacent Railway Junction Inn *(see page 142.*

Luckily, the Company had other sites already. Early on, they had leased three further mills in the area, West Mill, Hyde Mill and Ickleford Mill, the last two eventually being purchased. Astwick had ceased production in 1922. Ickleford Mill was now a large, ultra-modern production facility, and in 1980, it was doubled in size. Meanwhile the Company had bought and modernised a mill at Whitley Bridge in North Yorkshire.

A view of Bowman's Mill, approaching Hitchin from the Cambridge Road railway bridge. The upper storey was added during the re-building in 1947, following a major fire. (Hitchin Museum)

Station Mill was closed in 1981, and in 1985, it was demolished and the site sold for development. So passed a well-known and much loved Triangle landmark. However, Bowman's tankers are still very much a part of the local scene, as production flourishes at Ickleford, sustained by a loyal and long-serving workforce.

B & Q built their DIY store on the site; Warren's Art Cards business backed on to B & Q, and an ex-employee remembers talk of a ghost on the premises, always accompanied by the smell of freshly-baked bread. B & Q has subsequently moved to a new site on one of the retail sites in Stevenage and Warrens has also gone.

The Walsworth Road pill-box was part of the defences of the town during the Second World War. Following the Dunkirk evacuations of July 1940, when a German invasion of Britain was widely expected, thousands of these pill–boxes (*below-* Hitchin Museum) were built across the country. Few now remain and those that do are protected by law. This particular example guarded the railway bridge – Bowman's Mill can be seen to the rear right – and has a gas detector in front of it. The Property Sale notice on the pill-box is a humorous message, reading *"This property for sale…A hot reception for Adolph (sic), garage space for Goering and Goebbels"*.

As we are moving down Walsworth Road in an orderly fashion, our next port-of-call should be the railway station, which played such a significant role in the development of the Triangle that was recalled in Chapter One. We now cross the road and progress towards the town centre.

80 and 81 Walsworth Road, John Willmott & Sons.

The building firm of John Willmott & Sons was an important presence on Walsworth Road for many years.

William John Willmott, the second of seven sons of an enterprising builder from Bassingbourne in Cambridgeshire arrived in Hitchin in 1878 looking for opportunities. His father, John Willmott, had sensibly apprenticed each of his sons either as a bricklayer or a carpenter, thus ensuring both their livelihoods and the continuity of the family business.

William bought out the successful business of Frederick Jeeves, in Trevor Road. *(see page 42)* in the early 1880s, and began work from his yard. Before long he purchased a field fronting Walsworth Road and built two terraces of villas. He moved into one of the houses (number 80) and proceeded to develop new business premises on the back of the field. He was still working in conjunction with his father, and was joined by a brother, Walter, hence the name "John Willmott and Sons".

The business soon expanded to include a large joinery shop (moved from Bassingbourne), which stood on wooden posts, a saw-pit, and a variety of new machinery which served to increase the speed and efficiency of the operations.

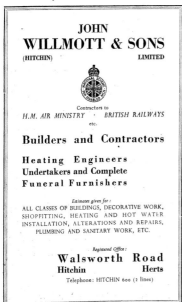

JOHN
WILLMOTT & SONS
(HITCHIN)   LIMITED

Contractors to
H.M. AIR MINISTRY · BRITISH RAILWAYS
etc.

Builders and Contractors

Heating Engineers
Undertakers and Complete
Funeral Furnishers

Estimates given for :
ALL CLASSES OF BUILDINGS, DECORATIVE WORK,
SHOPFITTING, HEATING AND HOT WATER
INSTALLATION, ALTERATIONS AND REPAIRS,
PLUMBING AND SANITARY WORK, ETC.

Registered Office :
Walsworth Road
Hitchin   Herts
Telephone: HITCHIN 600 (2 lines)

An advertisement from the Hitchin Directory of 1948. At this time, the firm also provided funeral services as well as its very valued building programme.

Important contracts were taken on locally, including much work for the Railway. Several large schools were built, including the very fine Hitchin Girls' Grammar School in 1908.

The Company had been re-formed in 1896, and William, Walter and another brother, Samuel, formed a branch at Hornsey in North London, thus opening up important opportunities in the capital. Joinery for all the projects was provided by the Hitchin yard to which an up-to-date machine shop had been added. The years following the First World War saw the business grow in size and reputation. It has always been served by generations of local craftsmen, some of whom have spent their entire working life with the firm. The wisdom of devolving skills down the generations has held for the owners themselves, and sons were apprenticed and trained in management skills, so that they, in turn, could direct the business.

In time, the Company formed separate branches, and ours became "John Willmott and Sons (Hitchin) Ltd". The founding brothers made their mark in the community. William John Willmott was a Justice of the Peace and became Chairman of Hitchin Urban District Council, of which his brother, Walter, was also a Member. During the Second World War, the Company was almost entirely engaged in contracts for the Air Ministry, a huge body of work, and in the years that followed, in improving and building new housing, both private and public.

At the beginning of the 1970s, Ian Dixon was appointed as a director, and was soon to become Managing Director. Under his guidance, the company grew still further, becoming widely recognised as one of the top privately owned construction firms in the U.K.

Although the offices at No 80 had been extended by the purchase of No 81, the company had outgrown all the available space. It was decided to re-locate to a new site in Queen Street, that of the former Congregational Church. That site was cleared and a new two-storey Head Office was built and occupied in 1971. Within a few years, the firm re-located again, bringing all its operations on to one site at Henlow, and after a presence in Hitchin of ninety-seven years, they moved out of town.

Today, the Company's former yard is a hive of industry of quite another sort. Tucked away, behind the bustle of the main road, are a number of successful small business enterprises. Seven units now occupy the space where William John Willmott set up his new venture in the 1880s. They are as varied as Graphics, Communications, Print Finishing, "Charisma Beads" and a busy Repair and Servicing Garage. Numbers 80 and 81 Walsworth Road are home to four Company Offices and a Studio.

Memories of 87 Walsworth Road, by Margaret and Bill Harmer and Valerie Taplin

Bill and Margaret remember Mrs Daphne Fisher, later Daphne Sellens, who was not only their landlady but over the years became their special friend. Bill and Margaret moved from South East London to Hitchin in 1960. They did

Daphne Sellens (previously Fisher) and Fred Sellens, probably on their wedding day, 1965 at Holy Saviour Church, Radcliffe Road (Margaret Harmer)

not have anywhere to live, so rented a room from Mrs Daphne Fisher at 87 Walsworth Road. Mrs Fisher was known as Daphne, but was born Gertrude Augusta Drieselman in the Transvaal, South Africa in 1885 to parents of Dutch origin. Her family was quite wealthy as they were diamond merchants and also owned several diamond mines. When the Boer War started, her parents sent her to boarding school and she did not return to her home for many years.

Daphne married a Harry Fisher, a well-known photographer in South Africa. They decided to move to England and brought most of their home with them including a white baby grand piano. Mrs Fisher continued to play the piano well into old age. They first lived in Corby in Northamptonshire and their three sons and two daughters were all born there. They eventually moved to Hitchin, to 87 Walsworth Road and the daughters attended the Girls' Grammar School. One daughter, Ruth, went back to South Africa in 1947 and the Harmers still keep in touch with her. Harry Fisher died on 14th February 1959 and Daphne married Fred Sellens in 1965 at Holy Saviour Church, Radcliffe Road.

In 1964, Margaret and Bill moved to a flat in Dacre Road and Daphne and Fred also moved to a flat in Radcliffe Road, as the house was too big for them. Margaret remembers her own children always calling Daphne Big Nana, to distinguish her from their own Nana.

Daphne died in the Lister Hospital, Stevenage on 4th November 1982, aged 93 years and Fred died soon afterwards. Margaret and Bill still keep in touch with the rest of the family.

Valerie Taplin remembers. "As a young girl I remember Daphne as what you might call "a lady with character". Daphne was a big tall lady and you always saw her wearing a big hat, gloves, large earrings and big necklaces and sometimes she wore a fox fur round her neck. This is something that would not go down too well today; she also always carried an umbrella. I was about eight years old and

Valerie Taplin (née Craft) on the left with Daphne Fisher's granddaughter, Barbara, right, outside 87 Walsworth Road in the early 1950s, "following a sunny day out in Clacton" (Valerie Taplin)

sometimes Daphne's granddaughter, Barbara, came to stay with her. I remember one day she took us to Clacton for the day and she bought us both a big sun hat. We had our photo taken on the side wall of No 87 Walsworth Road. In 1952 we moved to Walsworth to live and did not see Daphne very much after that. She was a lady that stood out in the crowd!"

88 Walsworth Road, "Alpha Villa"

Alpha Villa was a substantial property, built for a farmer, named Thomas Hall in the mid-1850s. Eventually the house was purchased by the Sanders family who owned the carriage and motor vehicle works on the opposite side of the road. They changed the name to "Desmond House", allegedly after a lucky bet on a racehorse named "Desmond"! Many of the elegant vehicles photographed for the firm's brochures were taken with the house wall as a backdrop.

In the 1960s, Desmond House was adapted for use as a petrol station, with a small kiosk and four small petrol pumps. The house was demolished when Walsworth Motor Co. took over the site to build a car showroom and accident and repair centre. In 2003, Walsworth Motor Co was in turn demolished and the

Alpha Villa in its reincarnation as a Petrol Station. (The late David Humphries)

site was sold to builders, Stephen Howard Homes to build blocks of flats and an underground car park. These are now named Sanders Place.

Hall's Wall

In 1855, Thomas Hall built this wall dividing Alpha Villa and Rose Cottage with a plaque on each side, leaving no doubt about the ownership! The wall still stands (*pictured right by* Valerie Taplin 2008)

89, Walsworth Road, "Rose Cottage "; "Rose Cottage Gardens"

One of the first and most desirable building plots to be sold off by the British Land Company was quickly snapped-up by John Douglas, a railway contractor.

He was described as "of Stowmarket" in 1845. We don't know exactly when the land was purchased, but it seems likely that by the mid 1850s "the very convenient and compact Residence" called "Rose Cottage" had been erected, "only about two minutes' walk from the Station". It would have stood in comparative isolation, only "Alpha Villa" and the Railway Inn standing on that side of the road in those days.

Photograph of Rose Cottage, from "The history of St Michael's and the Catholic Parish of Hitchin" (Hitchin Museum)

The "Kitchen and Pleasure Gardens" were enhanced by two large heated greenhouses, and the convenience of a two-stall stable and a carriage house. This was clearly a "Gentlemen's Residence", although John Douglas had only a brief tenure, dying in 1857. His widow had a tenant installed, soon to become well-known in the town.

Charles Archibald Bartlett was one of our early "commuters", drawn to the town by the new railway. He was a wholesale bookseller, with a business in Paternoster Square in the City of London. He moved here with his wife Lucy, and soon became involved with charitable causes in Hitchin. He was a member of the Independent Chapel in Dead (Queen) Street, and worked tirelessly for the welfare of the poor. He had always intended to build a house for himself, and before long bought a plot in Highbury Road, where he commissioned a villa not unlike "Rose Cottage". Bartlett was present in Walsworth Road on the 1861 census, but had moved on by 1866.

Hot on his heels came the Misses Feltham. They were a pair of Quaker ladies of "independent means", who had been living at home with a widowed father in the census of 1861, in a north London suburb. Following his death, they had even more "means" and set up home at "Rose Cottage" with two female servants. As members of the Religious Society of Friends, they would have been made welcome by their fellow Quakers and may well have already had connections in the town. Miss Mary Feltham died in 1877; her younger sister moved to a large house in Bancroft, where she was joined by a maiden aunt and "Rose Cottage" once more needed an occupant.

This set the stage for the arrival of one of the house's more notable owners. Mrs Elizabeth Lucas was the second wife of the Quaker artist Samuel Lucas who lived at "The Tilehouse" in Tilehouse Street. He died in 1865, leaving his widow and her two step-daughters in occupation. The widow was no "shrinking violet",

The signed portrait which was the frontispiece to Elizabeth Lucas' "Collected poems" published by Headley Brothers in 1900 (John Lucas)

but a lady of determined character and independent means. She was a member of a prominent Quaker family even before she married Samuel. She also had considerable literary pretensions, publishing poems and articles in genteel magazines and journals. Following Maria Feltham's removal to Bancroft, Mrs Lucas bought "Rose Cottage" and lived there for twenty years.

Her time there seems to have been both happy and successful. "Living on own means" with "income from leases of residences", she was clearly well-to-do, and her verses gained in popularity. She was included in an anthology of "Quaker Poets of Great Britain and Ireland" published during her lifetime in 1896, and a collection of her poems appeared following her death in 1899. One, titled "Our Pets at Rose Cottage" gives a flavour of her life there, and although rather too florid for modern tastes, hints at a life full of secluded charm and acts as a counterbalance to the rather intimidating portrait!

OUR PETS AT ROSE COTTAGE

SWEET-BRIER, our good mare, must lead
   the train,
In coat of glossy bay and jet-black mane.
So free to start, heeds not the freight behind,
Always for speed, o'er hill and dale, inclined,
So light of foot, along our flowery lanes,
And gentlest, when a lady holds the reins.

Next comes in age, in honour and in fame,
Wolsey, august, the Cardinal, his name,
Smoke hued, black face and paws, eyes green
   and mild,
Heavy to lift and carried like a child.
Sleeps on his mistress' couch, a ball of fur,
And wakes to greet her with his sweetest
   purr.
It happened to our hero, once, that he
A squirrel spied on our big cherry tree.
With chattering teeth and eager upturned
   eyes
Wolsey beheld this all entrancing prize.
From bough to bough he crept, but all
   in vain,
That branch beyond could ne'er his
   weight sustain.
Well pleased, we watched our squirrel,
   leaping, fly

To neighbouring trees that waved against
   the sky.

Next, see the Lady Jeremiah sail,
With slow and stately step and
   feathered tail,
Her kitten's nest she made in a deep box,
Withal to hide it from that sly
   young fox –
The Dandy Dinmont, whose pet name
   by turns
Is Robin, Robbie, sometimes
   Robert Burns.
In figure, as in voice, he's long and loud,
And of his ginger curls we're justly proud;
Nor can we e'er dispute the fact that he
Our "Robin Goodfellow" is bound to be.

Next, youthful Felix, gentlest of his race,
And not without full tail and Tabby grace.
See! To his mistress' lap, he quickly glides,
There for a little space in quiet hides,
Emerges soon, looks bold and sly and then
Ends with a raid upon her ink and pen.
Whether to write his life he then desired
(But if he did, the fact has not transpired),
Or to indite the lines above supplied,
We leave our gentle reader to decide

E.S.L. (OR FELIX).

From a selection of poems by Elizabeth S. Lucas. (Felix is the cat!)

Elizabeth Lucas died in February 1899, at the age of 83, and by June of the same year her Executors had placed "Rose Cottage" on the market. Walsworth Road had become much busier since the opening–up of Hermitage Road in 1878, and the house was no longer a villa on the leafy outskirts of the town.

The buyer was the "self-made" Uriah Brooksbank, who had moved down from Selby in Yorkshire with his wife Susan. Elizabeth Lucas might possibly have shuddered, as the £1,625 handed over by Mr Brooksbank , described as a "wholesale fruit and vegetable merchant" (employer) on the 1881 census, was therefore "trade"! Uriah Brooksbank died in 1902, leaving his wife in possession of the property. She outlived him by only three years, so, in 1905 "Rose Cottage" was vacant once again.

The next mention of a tenant is intriguing. In the 1906 edition of Kelly's Directory, the occupant is listed as "Convent of the Sacred Heart. (Rev. Mother Mary Theresia)". In 1905 a "teaching sister" joined the group of French Catholic Sisters running the laundry in Nightingale Road, with the intention of setting-up both a parochial school and a convent. The vacant "Rose Cottage" seemed to have provided an ideal starting location, well away from the thriving laundry. The school began with three pupils, but rapidly expanded, and by the time the lease expired in late 1907, the single sister had been joined by several more, and a lay-teacher. It was time to move on. (see *page 84* for a fuller account of the Sacred Heart Convent in Hitchin).

William Haysom bought the property when the school went. Sadly, local directories whose information we have been forced to fall back on, don't tell us anything about him or his family. He is listed as the occupier until at least 1922, and possibly longer, and by now "Rose Cottage" had the number "89" as an additional identity.

In 1926 the property was bought by a family whose clothiers' business still thrives in Bucklersbury. George Hawkins made the house his family home for the next thirty years. Following George's death, his widow continued to live at "No 89", as it was now numbered, until the end of the 1950s.

Mr G.D. Buckley and his family subsequently bought the house, and are listed there in 1969. In 1972 the local firm of accountants, Bradshaw Johnson, were seeking to expand their operations. Walsworth Road was increasingly seen as an area of business opportunity, and No.89 offered both space, and good parking facilities. They moved into the house in 1973, and remained on-site for over thirty years. Inevitably, the character of the property altered to suit its new purpose. Modifications to the original house had already taken place over the past century, and now internal alterations removed many of the features that the early residents would have cherished. In 2006, driven by the inexorable tide of development washing down the road, the house was bought by developers, Michael Shanley Homes and application was sought to demolish it and replace it with a close of ten town houses and three apartments. Despite a valiant campaign led by local groups and individuals, planning permission was granted in February 2007, and the site was cleared in July and August that year. "Rose Cottage Gardens" took the place of "Rose Cottage", completed in June 2009.

One wonders, do the new residents half-hear the sound of Sweet Brier's hooves on the carriage sweep, and the gentle rumble of the carriage wheels?

An account of the building now accommodating Paul's Cycles, formerly Frost's appears in Trevor Road, as the building was originally connected with Day's market gardens in that road.

96 Walsworth Road, Esther Fuller, *née* Cannon

Esther Cannon was born in 1849, the youngest of five children of parents George and Mary. Her father was a master baker and her mother a housekeeper. In 1851 the family was living and baking in Bancroft Street where they stayed for the next forty years or so. George, died in June 1870, aged fifty seven, but his widow, Mary and her daughters continued to run the bakery. They had a lodger, Frank Fuller, also a baker, whom Esther married in 1873. A baby daughter, Mary, sadly died in 1874, just five months old. Baking was obviously in the blood and they wanted it to continue, as they took in another boarder, also a baker.

Esther's mother, Mary, died in 1889, aged eighty and by 1891, Arthur and Esther had moved to a new house and shop at 96 Walsworth Road, Hitchin, taking with them Esther's sister, Maria and two servants.

Arthur Frank Fuller died in 1902, aged fifty three, but Esther lived on until 19th October 1928. They never had any more children after their daughter died and all three are buried in the same plot in Hitchin Cemetery in St John's Road.

Interestingly, two further occupants of No 96 were also bakers, **Angel's** (1926) and **W.J. Stevens** (1937) (Hitchin Directories). Other later businesses at 96 and 97 were **Bottoms & Co,** makers and purveyors of Benledi bicycles and gramophones and **Darkers,** French polishers.

David Binks, a much respected undertaker, occupied the premises until his retirement where once Darker's furniture was bought, sold and exchanged. The premises retain his name but is now run by Neville's of Luton.

110 Walsworth Road, "Omega House"

This substantial corner- house, was purpose-built for its owner, Frederick Jeeves' retirement; presumably this accounted for the "Omega" name, being his last residence. Its distinctive "barley-sugar-twist" chimneys are the only ones remaining in Hitchin. Frederick, a builder, late of Trevor Road, *(see page 42)*, sold out to John Willmott & Sons in the early 1880s. He enjoyed it for many years, dying in 1910. The 1891 census described him as "retired builder...living on own means". Following his death, his unmarried daughter, Lizzie Jeeves, lived there until 1953.

"Teletubbies" in the Triangle

Having arrived back where we started at the junction with Verulam Road and Highbury Road, we are confronted by a modern roundabout.

Ellie Clarke, Secretary, Hitchin Forum (1994-2008) remembers its first appearance.

"Walsworth Road has always offered a pleasant approach into the town centre, so when it became obvious in 1999, that major highway works were to be carried out to make its junction with Verulam Road safer, local activists took an interest. Here was an opportunity to create an attractive space, fitting for the boundary of Hitchin's Conservation Area.

The "interest" became a full-blown campaign when a roundabout like no other in Hitchin was built. First of all, 3 mature trees were chopped down to improve driver 'sight-lines'. Then high granite kerbs (nice touch that!) were constructed, enclosing a mound covered in black and white chevrons, surmounted by 4 chubby plastic bollards. It rapidly became known as the 'teletubbies' roundabout.

After a year of protests, presentations, letters and safety reviews, the teletubbies climbed down to make way for more conventional signs. However, campaigners never did manage to persuade the highway engineers that floral planting or a Hitchin-themed sculpture would be more appropriate."

Chapter  3

Trevor Road

This road was built on a parcel of land known as Little Benslow Hills, owned by William Wilshere, the prominent local 19th century lawyer. Most of the little cul-de-sac was developed between 1880 and the turn of the 20th Century, although the first houses came in the 1860s. The road appears to be named after Thomas Trevor of Kimpton Hoo, also known as Whitwell or Walden Hoo. He stood for Parliament in 1852 on an anti-corn law ticket. Although the Corn Laws had been abolished, there was a movement for their return which Thomas Trevor and others wished to oppose.

A mixture of large detached and semi-detached houses and a row of terraced cottages have been built in Trevor Road over the last 150 years. The first houses were built in 1864; Mr William Bray, a wheelwright and Baptist Minister from Walkern, bought two plots of land from the estate of Walter Elliott Whittingham. The plots were sold by public auction at the Sun Hotel for £80 and £82 respectively. William Bray built three houses on the plots, now numbered 5, 6 and 7, the latter known as Trevor House and including a private Baptist Chapel.

1886

No 7 was sold to Mary Featherstonehaugh, wife of Henry Gascoigne Featherstonehaugh, for £1,250. It is also likely that William Bray sold Nos 5 and 6 around the same time, although he is still recorded as living in No 7 in 1886. No 5 was occupied by Miss Micklejohn and No 6 by George Russell the younger.

1908

No 5 was divided into apartments and managed by Mrs Annie Ashford who lived in the basement. The house at this time was owned by Susan Bird, the wife of the Minister at Walsworth Road Baptist Church. She also had a toyshop in Walsworth Road.

1938

No 5 was occupied by the two unmarried Wilshere sisters, Hilda Ada and Mabel. Their father had bought it for £365 from Ruth Macdonald and Dorothy Louise Cooper, probably sisters who had inherited it from Susan Bird. They may have been her daughters. Mary Else at No 13 recalls the Wilshere sisters taking a great interest in all their neighbours and giving them sweets at Christmas.
It is thought Nos 9 and 10, originally one house, were also built in the 1860's. The 1881 map shows a large building at the top of Trevor Road on the eastern side, where Nos 9 and 10 are now, No 8 being an Edwardian infill.

In 1863, a parcel of land was transferred to Alfred Ransom of Bancroft Street and later Benslow House. Alfred Ransom is described in the 1871 census as "Farmer… and brick and lime manufacturer", both occupations employing a considerable workforce. He lived in a large house in Bancroft at that time and his lime kilns were at Benslow above the station area. As the piece of land now occupied by No 11 was also in the ownership of the Ransom family for many years, it seems likely that the parcel transferred in 1863 included all of the top end of the road, bordering onto the footpath now called Burtons Path. The 1871 and 1881 census records do not list house numbers, so it is a matter of deduction as to which houses the records refer. The residents' occupations are listed, however and one William F. Morris, Minister of the Gospel, is occupying one house with his children, a boarder and a servant. It is fair to assume that this was Nos 9 and 10, as he and his family were there in 1891. By 1901, the house had been divided as William Morris and family were now at No 10 and No 9 was occupied by William B. Alexander, a retired chemist and his daughter.

By 1911, No 10 was a boarding house and Margaret Sophy Brown was boarding- house keeper. Apparently there used to be a communicating door between these two houses which was still there in the 1980s when the houses had been turned into bedsitters. Noel Arthur Barre took possession in 1919 and Captain Bertram Shillitoe, master mariner in 1922. John Myatt who until recently ran his musical instruments shop in Nightingale Road, *(see page 111)* bought No 10 in 1956 where he started the Cellar Press, later run by his son, Peter. After John Myatt moved to St Bridget's in Radcliffe Road, the house became a hotel, run by Messrs Guiseppi and Domenico Guddami: it then passed to Alan Eric Michel and in 1983, was bought by Malcolm and Janet Hicks.

No 8 is listed for the first time in 1901 so must have been built during the previous decade. It was occupied by Albert E. Austin, clergyman of the Church of England.

No 11, also known as St Bernard's does not appear on an 1881 map but it is visible on an 1898 one. In 1911, it was occupied by Juliet Grace, a widow and in 1912 was conveyed to her by her sister Priscilla Ransom, so the house may well have been built by the Ransom family.

It is not clear how long she lived there herself, as Lucy Hensley rented it from 1926 for 5 years at an annual rent of £40. When Juliet Grace died in 1929, she left all of her real estate to her sister, Priscilla and brother, Theodore, and in 1930, Theodore conveyed his share to Priscilla. She died in 1935 and it was bought from her estate by

Sketch of the plot then occupied by No 11, "St Bernard's", in 1912 (Jeremy and Renate Burrowes from their house deeds)

Numbers 3-10, Trevor Road, circa 1926. (David and Jenny Shirley)

Clara Anne Creasey for £850. After her death in 1947, it was bequeathed to her niece Minnie Constance Creasey of Knebworth, who sold it in 1954 to James Ellis and Florence Gorham for £2,800. James died in 1958 and his widow, Florence then sold it to Dennis Pollock Ltd for £3,500. It was then, successively a guest house and nursing home until bought by the Burrowes family in 1995. It was in this house that Renate Burrowes started her Kindersmill Day Nursery, now in Grove Road.

It is thought that Nos 2 -4 are of an early date as are most of the houses on the opposite side of the road, except for Nos 19 and 20 which are a later infill. In 1871, the house occupied by the Jeeves family must have been either No 1 or 2 or both. Frederick Jeeves, was cousin to the successful Queen Street builder, George Jeeves and initially worked for him. By 1871, he had set up on his own account, with a house and yard in Trevor Road. Ten years later he was described as "builder, employing 25 men", still living at the same address. This was a successful company, responsible for major contracts in the town. In the 1880s Frederick sold his business to John Wilmott & Sons and moved to Omega House, No 110 Walsworth Road, which he had built for himself on the corner of Highbury Road. *(see page 39)*

In 1886, No 2 was occupied by Henry Brown, town missionary and from 1902 to 1906 by Hannah Underwood, dressmaker. The yard backing onto Rose Cottage in Walsworth Road was owned by William Anderson and went with 2 Trevor Road. (No 1 was part of the Rose Cottage estate.)William Anderson built Nos 3 and 4 on this yard and various members of the Cotton family lived at Nos 2, 3 and 4.

Vimy Cotton was named by her father after Vimy Ridge as he was away fighting in the First World War when she was born. She lived with her mother at No 2 and her elder brother Eric, born in 1913, worked in the yard. Their father,

A wonderful aerial view of 3–8 Trevor Road in the 1980s. No 7, the right hand house of the three white ones, shows the extension where the Baptist Chapel was. To the rear are the Rose Cottage stables and conservatory at the back of Cotton's Yard. (David and Jenny Shirley)

he of the Vimy Ridge, was a painter and decorator and worked from the yard, but he also ran The Junction public house in Nightingale Road (since demolished).

In 1911, Nos 12, 13 and 14 were sold by auction at the Sun Hotel and bought by Miss Rose Anderson for £510. Her descendants still owned them until 2008. It was to No 13 that Mary Else, aged 10 months came to live with her parents and she still lives in the same house. Mary was born in 1923 in the lodge house of Ransom's in Bancroft. When she left school, she first worked for the Spirella Company in Letchworth, as many young women did in those days, but spent the rest of her working life as a typist.

Cotton and Day "Decorators etc" as painted on the Yard entrance door at No 2, Trevor Road. (Hitchin Museum)

No 13 is now owned by a distant relative of Mary Else. One of Mary's great friends is Leslie Dargert (*née* Bullard) an artist well-recorded in her book "A walk around Hitchin in pictures".

At the same auction in 1911, Nos 15 and 16 were bought by Mr Christopher Anderson for £330, Nos 17 and 18 by Mr Adam Hill, dentist, for £360 and Nos 3 and 4 by Mr A. Clarke for £380, all part of the late Mr William Anderson's estate. But five of them at least stayed in the Anderson family.

From the 1880s, on the corner of Trevor Road and Walsworth Road, there stood the Temperance Hotel owned by Simeon and Eliza Leete and subsequently by their daughter. It was much used by cyclists. It was quite a large site and when the hotel closed, was divided up into separate buildings in 1953 by Mr Frost the elder, who had the bicycle shop. Part of Frost's original shop is now Paul's Cycles. Philip Day had previously owned what became Mr Frost's shop; he had a greengrocery business there and grew his produce in gardens at the top of Trevor Road. He eventually gave up the gardens where garages were built and now three modern town houses stand next to No 11 at the top of the road. He continued with his shop for some time afterwards, however.

Triangle "native" Derek Wheeler has memories of both Frost's Cycle Shop and of the neighbourhood in the 1960s.

"In the autumn of 1967, by way of a slump in family fortunes, three Wheelers, mother and father and myself, found themselves homeless, and by the rapid revolution of the wheel of fortune, soon found themselves living in a very comfortable, indeed, bespoke, abode.

The late Charlie Frost and his wife Hazel (recently deceased), kindly rented us the flat above the Frost's cycle shop in Walsworth Road. I must say that the year I spent there was one of the happiest in my life. Since I had a collection of Victorian bicycles to store and restore, the Frost backyard, where I was allowed to keep my workbench and tools, was an ideal environment wherein to pursue a hobby, although Mrs Day who lived above the fruiterer's shop next door was heard to remark in her own inimitable fashion, after a particularly long period of enduring me using a five-pint brazing blowlamp.

'He's either making a noise or a smell, that boy'

The Frosts encouraged my eccentric behaviour and I got on particularly well with an elderly neighbour of theirs, from Trevor Road, called Fred Bullard. Whenever I got home from teaching at Queen Street School, Fred would be in the cycle workshop talking to Charlie about the state of

Frost's cycle shop on the corner of Walsworth Road and Trevor Road, 2005. It is now Paul's cycles, a smaller shop fronting Walsworth Road only. (Ashley Walker)

Britain and whether or not Mrs such-and-such should really be allowed out on her own! He always left at the shop's closing time, leaving a trail of tobacco smoke behind him and loudly murmuring that he was going to have kippers and custard again for tea today! Fred's daughter is the talented Lesley Dargert.

Graham Frost was at this time still at school but I have known him since he was five years old, being a friend of a young cousin of mine.

Charles Frost set up in business in Bridge Street in Hitchin in 1953, when there were at least half a dozen cycle shops in the town. The shop moved to its present site at 94 Walsworth Road, in 1959. It expanded to take in the adjacent shop in 1971, and in 1989 enlarged its premises again to provide a new workshop, and a clothing department. Charlie's son, Graham, joined the family business in 1977, and after the death of his father in 1983, Graham took on Paul Bullen as his business partner".

(These memories are part of an article written by Derek in 2003 for the Hitchin Historical Society "Hitchin Journal" of which he was editor at the time)

In August 2005, Paul's Cycles opened in the part of the building fronting Walsworth Road; Paul Bullen, head mechanic and manager of the original C J Frost's business now continues the tradition of the building which has for so long favoured cyclists.

Trevor Road is a small road and a close, so there is a feeling of cosiness and community about it and a recent young arrival is known to be very pleased with the welcome from neighbours and the Triangle community. It is evident from Mary Else's memories that this neighbourliness dates from earlier times too. She herself organized a street party for VJ Day in 1945 and has kindly lent a photograph of the happy occasion. *(See page 46)*

Trevor Road street party for VJ Day 1945. "VJ" stands for "Victory in Japan", the ultimate strategic victory achieved by the Allies in 1945. Mary Else is standing front left in her picture and she also provided a list of those who attended the street party, written in her own hand.

1   Tom Pettingell
2   Fred Bullard
3   Mr Book
4   Mrs Lewis
5   Mrs Pull
6   Dolly Lee
7   Maggie Stallobrass
8   Mr Greg (Friend of above)
9   Arthur West
10 Carol Stallerbrass (daughter of Bonnie)
11 Mrs Stallerbrass (Mother of Maggie + Bonnie)
12 Mr Percy Franklin
13 Edith Cartwright ⎫
14 Lessie   "   ⎬ sisters
15 Vimy Cotter
16 Mrs Cotter (Mother of Vimy)
17 Michael Cotton (Son of Eric + Rachel Cotter)

STANDING
18 Mary Else   21 Gertrude Franklin
19 Doris Pettingell   22 Florence Else
20 Hazel Ranson

46

Chapter 4

Radcliffe Road

In the 19th Century, land known as Twelve Acres was owned by Thomas Brown. According to records and the 1844 map, part of this land was split into three fields in which corn may have grown; two of the fields were occupied by William Bowyer and the third by William Hall. Radcliffe Road and Dacre Road were formed from this parcel of land. Radcliffe Road was built about 1857 and named after the Radcliffe Family, later the Delmé Radcliffe Family, who owned Hitchin Priory from the 16th century until 1963. The Church of the Holy Saviour in Radcliffe Road is the only Grade II listed building in the Triangle. The church and the other buildings founded by the Reverend George Gainsford still dominate the road, surrounded as they are by the terraced cottages built mainly to house the railway workers, and one or two larger dwellings.

The Gainsford Family

The Reverend George Gainsford who founded and was the first vicar of Holy Saviour Church in Radcliffe Road, could trace his family back to the 1300s. George's father, George Richard Gainsford was a linen draper and had two children, George, born 1829 and Augusta. When George Richard died in 1861, he left £60,000 to be divided equally between his two children which may explain why George Gainsford could afford to build a church from his personal income as well as being a generous benefactor in the town of Hitchin.

George went to school in Brighton, then to King's College, Cambridge and Pembroke College, Oxford. He was ordained at 23 years of age and took up his first curacy at St Mary's, Hitchin, in 1852. During the two years there, he was largely instrumental in the building of the original St Andrew's School at the bottom of Hollow Lane. A tablet inside the school read "Erected mainly through the exertions of the Rev. George Gainsford, Curate of this Parish, MDCCCLIV (1854). He married the vicar's daughter, Annette Wiles, in 1854 and after another curacy in Kent and an incumbency in Cheshire he and Annette returned to Hitchin in 1863. He had decided to devote his wealth to building and endowing a church and settled on Hitchin as the location. Maybe his wife was anxious to return to her previous home? The building of the Holy Saviour Church started in Radcliffe Road in 1864.

They had a house built on a plot of land in Walsworth Road, called "Woodside", now a car park and the site of the Queen Mother Theatre. Until this house was ready, they lived, at least for some of the time, in Elm Lodge in Upper Tilehouse

GAINSFORD FAMILY TREE

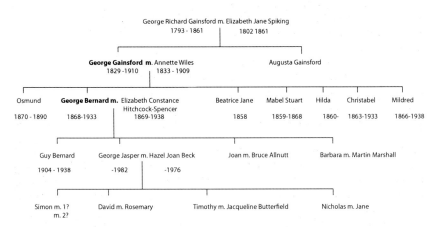

George Richard Gainsford m. Elizabeth Jane Spiking
1793 - 1861 / 1802 1861

George Gainsford m. Annette Wiles / Augusta Gainsford
1829 -1910 / 1833 - 1909

Osmund / **George Bernard m.** Elizabeth Constance Hitchcock-Spencer / Beatrice Jane / Mabel Stuart / Hilda / Christabel / Mildred
1870 - 1890 / 1868-1933 / 1869-1938 / 1858 / 1859-1868 / 1860- / 1863-1933 / 1866-1938

Guy Bernard / George Jasper m. Hazel Joan Beck / Joan m. Bruce Allnutt / Barbara m. Martin Marshall
1904 - 1938 / -1982 / -1976

Simon m. 1? m. 2? / David m. Rosemary / Timothy m. Jacqueline Butterfield / Nicholas m. Jane

Street. The film script to "Tales of Tilehouse Street", made by the Hitchin Ciné Society, quotes from a lecture by Reginald Hine in 1941 describing their life there.

"…In the summer there were croquet parties, but croquet was not always the demure Victorian game that we are prone to think it. On one occasion, Mrs Gainsford picked up one of the croquet balls and flung it, in play, at the head of the Rev. Benjamin Parker, one of her husband's curates. It struck him in the eye and blinded him forever. There were Sunday School treats in the garden too, and very uproarious and unsanctified they were. One hears of Mr Gainsford making his way with difficulty into the house minus both coat tails.

In the evenings there were more or less innocent card games…concerts also and dances…Gainsford himself was a graceful dancer, a singer and something of a musician. It is said that the simple tune to the evening hymn 'Now the day is over' was composed by him as a lullaby, whilst he walked up and down the night nursery, with little Osmund in his arms".

In 1867, they moved into "Woodside", their newly-built home. This was a large and gracious-looking house, almost certainly designed by William Butterfield, the architect of Holy Saviour Church. The diaper-patterned brickwork was characteristic of Butterfield's work and an entry on the Royal Institute of British Architects' on-line library catalogue includes 'Hitchin parsonage' in a volume of his work.

The 1881 census recorded sixteen people living there.

George Gainsford's churchmanship was of the High Church kind, the Oxford Movement being strong during the time he was a student there. In 1904, he had to defend himself against a charge of popery by a 'spy' from the Ecclesiastical Commission. He had very strict views and had no time for the Salvation Army or the Church Army, but was a kind and sincere Christian. He believed literally in the Bible and always preached sermons based on the gospel.

Mr and Mrs Gainsford lived as many upper middle class Victorians, with servants, but exerted themselves for the benefit of others. Mrs Gainsford visited the workhouse weekly, organized a fund for it at Christmas, provided entertainment at New Year and an outdoor treat at "Woodside" during the summer. She took a full part in organisations such as the Girls' Friendly Society, Mothers' Meeting at Holy Saviour, helped in the Sunday School and visited St Saviour's School weekly. She was especially concerned with missions and was well-known in the orphanage and almshouses, including the Biggin and the Bancroft ones, the North and South Herts Hospitals and St Luke's Home of Rest. She walked everywhere in the town; was this unusual for a lady of those times? In an article in the church magazine of 1913, Arthur Allison calls her the "sweet mother of our parish".

The couple had their Golden Wedding on 20th April 1904 and typically, a lot of their presents were for the benefit of the church.

The Register of Services at Holy Saviour has the following account of George's funeral in 1910:-

"At 7.30 a.m. the body was conveyed from "Woodside" to St Saviour's for celebration of Holy Communion which was celebrated by his son George Bernard Gainsford; ...At 11 a.m. the burial office was recited to a full church. The route of

*The Reverend George Gainsford, aged 35, the year after the dedication of his Church of the Holy Saviour in Radcliffe Road. The posed portrait, complete with cane and dog is the essence of the respected Victorian gentleman. (*Hitchin Museum)

the procession was lined with people and there were huge crowds at the cemetery. The procession was headed by the cross bearer and included a number of children from the orphanage, with churchwardens, sidesmen, Sunday School teachers, Guild members and many others".

George and Annette Gainsford had five daughters, Beatrice, Mabel, Hilda, Christabel and Mildred, followed by two sons, George Bernard, born 1868 who followed his father into the church and Osmund, born 1870, who sadly died in 1890.

George Bernard went to Pembroke College, Oxford, like his father and Ely Theological College. He was ordained in Ely Cathedral in 1891. His first curacy was at St Paul's, Bedford after which he returned to be his father's curate at Holy Saviour and took over as vicar on his father's death in 1910.

Whereas his father had been mostly concerned with his parish and charitable works, George Bernard was a man of modern and varied activities. He joined the Hitchin Urban District Council in 1901, became vice-chairman in 1924 and chairman from 1925-28. He sat on various sub-committees, was a Guardian of the poor and a member of the Guardian's Committee for 28 years. Like his mother, he was a regular visitor to the workhouse and infirmary, was Chairman

The Reverend George Gainsford, photographed in extreme old age (he died in 1910). The location is something of a mystery, but is probably the South Garden of Holy Saviour Church. An 'old girl' of St Saviour's School remembers that there was an iron cross there which may be the object behind him. It bears a tantalizingly unreadable inscription. If the photograph was taken in the church garden, it is not a gravestone, as there has never been a churchyard. The chair looks very like the 'throne'-type chairs still in use in the Church by clergy and readers. (Original photograph given to the churchwardens in 2009. Origin unknown)

of the Managers of St Saviour's Schools and Trustee of the Orphanage and Almshouses. While at Oxford, he had joined G (Hitchin) Company the 1st Herts Volunteer Battalion as sub-lieutenant under the captain, his friend, J.H.Gilbertson, of the well-known doctor's family in Hitchin. In 1893, on his return to Hitchin, he took charge of the Company's cycling section and became chaplain to the Company. He formed the St Saviour's Church Lads' Brigade in 1904

His other interests were music and drama, being a founder member of the Hitchin Amateur Light Opera Company, later to become the Thespians, became President and was the first stage manager. He also took part in the St Saviour's Players' productions. How pleasing that the Bancroft Players built the Queen Mother Theatre on part of the grounds of his old family home. He was also something of a sportsman, rowing while at Oxford and playing football for Hitchin Town on a few occasions. He was one of the first in Hitchin to own a motor car and was a member of North Herts Motoring Club. He was often to be seen riding on the footplate of a locomotive and on one occasion was a war- time coal driver.

He was much loved, both as vicar and man and the following 'guessing poem' sums him up:-

"A resonant voice and sonorous
He always takes care not to bore us
His sermons are short
But contain all they ought
And he's awfully good at a chorus"

Attributed to Smith Major, alias Mrs A.W. Thomas. Who are they? Hitchin Notabilities, Bancroft Press, 1920 and reprinted from St Saviour's Choir Journal.

George Bernard and 'Else', as his wife was known, had two sons, Guy Bernard and George Jasper and two daughters, Joan and Barbara. During George Bernard's curacy, he lived at St Katharine's in Verulam Road and after his marriage, moved into "Birchfield" next door and then to "Woodside" in 1906. He died suddenly on 18th February 1933 aged 65. The Herts Express dedicated a whole page tribute on Saturday, 25th February.

Guy, the younger son, was apparently an all-round sportsman and had the "travel bug". He went to Asia and died tragically from cancer while there. As Jasper had no inclination for the ministry, the Gainsford 'dynasty' at Holy Saviour Church came to an end with George Bernard's death and vicars were appointed from outside.

George Bernard's wife, 'Else', who died in 1938, was something of an artist, it seems. She painted the scenery for the first production of the Hitchin Amateur Light Opera Company.

"An artist with waving dark hair
She looks like a girl I declare
With a daughter of twenty
And duties in plenty
So youthful a mien is most rare"

Just before George Bernard's death," Woodside" was found to be badly affected by woodworm and dry rot, so plans were drawn up for a new house to replace it, pulling down "Woodside" and bequeathing the land to the people of Hitchin. George Bernard's death so unexpectedly and his wife's five years later meant the new house was not built, but "Woodside" was demolished and the land taken over by the local Council.

George Jasper Gainsford, like his father, only ever known by his second name, also went to Oxford and studied theology at Lancing College, before deciding not to go into the Ministry. He was a cavalry officer in the First World War, but contracted rheumatic fever, making him unfit for service in the Second World War. The family was stationed in Norfolk and he was a member of the Royal Observer Corps, spotting incoming enemy planes.

The Reverend George Bernard Gainsford and his wife "Else" in their Aerial Quadricycle. He was a very keen motorist, being one of the first in Hitchin to own a car. It is not known where the picture is taken. (Nick and Jane Gainsford)

At the time of his marriage to Hazel Beck, Jasper was a motor engineer and proprietor of a garage in Berkshire, but he returned with his wife to Hitchin and set up home in "Birchfield" in Verulam Road in 1929, where their four sons grew up. Jasper and Hazel later moved into Number 35 Verulam Road, a house called Green Shutters. Jasper was also graced with a 'guessing poem'.

"Our joy at his birth was unbounded
We remember how gay the bells sounded
Now our ruddy-faced youth
Is a soldier, forsooth
And a gentleman growed! We're astounded"

Obviously inheriting his father's love of the motor car, Jasper had a driving school, the Birchfield School of Motoring and used a Morris Minor, registration number FLY 607. Before that, he had been one of the first AA support motorcyclists. At one time, he also drove chassis for Bentley, a perilous task which involved sitting on an orange box and driving just the chassis with no outer car body, from the factory to whoever was to make up the body and fittings!

Marriage of the Reverend George Bernard Gainsford to Elizabeth Constance Hitchcock-Spencer, known as 'Else', in June 1894 at St Saviour's Church. The service was conducted mostly by the groom's father, the Reverend George Gainsford. The two pages seated at the front were Bruce Allnutt, nephew of the groom and Marshall Gilbertson who later became a Hitchin G.P. Standing left to right: the bridegroom, Miss Gainsford?, the bride, Christabel Gainsford?, S.G.Davis, best man and college friend of the groom, Ethel Spencer?, Beatrice Hall? It was thought there were about 800 people in the church in addition to the invited guests and the road outside was also full of onlookers. The reception was held at Odsey Grange, Ashwell, the home of the bride's parents. (George Bernard's sister, Mildred, married William Edward Hitchcock Spencer, Else's brother) (Hitchin Museum)

One of Jasper's memories from childhood was of attending the same kindergarten in Dacre Road as the Queen Mother. He always said that if he'd known she was going to be Queen he may have paid her more attention!

Hazel Gainsford died in 1976 and Jasper survived until 1982.

Of Jasper and Hazel's four sons, David and Tim are sadly now deceased, but one, Nick, lives in Meppershall and his brother, Simon, is in Manila in the Philippines

The family has left a considerable memory behind; "Gainsford Crescent" immortalizes them as well as Gainsford Court.

Holy Saviour Church

At the beginning, the church was known as St Saviour's, although the Herts Express newspaper alternates the name with the Church of the Holy Saviour, its present name, in its various reports in 1865. We shall call it Holy Saviour for the sake of consistency. It was built as a thanksgiving for recovery from illness by the Rev. George Gainsford. He financed the building of the church and chose as architect William Butterfield of Adam Street, Adelphi, London, who was well known in the High Church tradition. All Saints', Margaret Street, London and the chapel of Keble College, Oxford, are fine examples of his work. By coincidence, the builder was the local firm of W. & H. Butterfield, unrelated to the renowned architect. The foundation stone was laid in May 1864 by Mrs Gainsford and the building was dedicated on Ascension Day, May 25th 1865 by the Bishop of Rochester. At this time Hitchin was in the Diocese of Rochester, St Albans not coming into being until 1877.

The establishment of this new parish by Queen in Council as reported in the London Gazette 1865, helped to serve the needs of a growing population between the town and the station since the arrival of the railway in 1850.

The following details are taken from the Monthly Advertiser June 1865 in its account of the dedication.

The Church is of Early Decorated design by W. Butterfield, consisting of chancel, chancel aisles, nave, north and south aisles, organ chamber and vestry.

It is built of red brick with Bath stone dressings, ornamented inside with incised patterns filled in with black cement. The roof is open and of stained deal and the aisles are paved with Minton's encaustic tiles… The whole contract was carried out by W.H.

The Church among the fields, 1865

From the Holy Saviour Church Centenary booklet, 1965

Butterfield, builders, and sub-contractors W. Seymour (seats), Franklin (painter & glazier), and Hinton (stone-mason) of Bedford. The total cost of building was about £2,900. The organ was donated by Miss Gainsford, sister of the incumbent and built by Mr Walker of London from a specification by W. Carling, organist of Hitchin, who played at the dedication and the Reverend Hensley preached the sermon. In the afternoon, all workmen

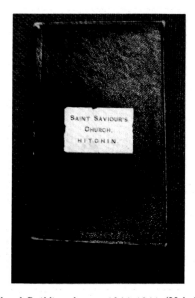

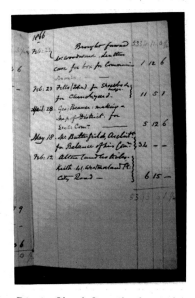

Church Building Account 1864-1866. (Holy Saviour District Church Council – deposited at Hertfordshire Archives and Local Studies)

concerned attended a dinner at the Swan Inn in the Market Place as guests of the Reverend George Gainsford.

The stained glass windows are of particularly good Victorian quality, most of them supplied by Messrs Hardman of Birmingham. By 1879, all windows had been replaced with stained glass except the clerestory ones. Many of them are dedicated to local notables or presented by members of the church. They were obviously planned in advance, as they tell the Bible story chronologically from Adam and Eve at the East end of the South aisle to the Crucifixion of Jesus at the East end of the North Aisle. The crowning glory is the East window behind the high altar, depicting the Ascension, designed by Alexander Gibb who had exhibited at the Great Exhibition of 1851. The East window was restored and re-leaded in 1977.

Externally, the church was surrounded by grass plots and gravel walks and enclosed by an iron fence. Early photographs show the church fronted by low brick walls with railings above, brick pillars and iron gates. The iron railings and gates were requisitioned during the war and have not been replaced, except for the gate to the north garden.

The seating capacity at the beginning was 400, but by 1880 it was necessary to build a new North aisle because of expanding congregations. In 1882 the congregation was still expanding and a new South aisle was built. The porch and the South East door were also added at this time. The capacity of the church was now nearly 1,000, but at Harvest Thanksgiving when the South aisle was dedicated, 1200 people attended and many were turned away.

In the latter part of the 19th Century and the beginning of the 20th, additions and enhancements to the building continued, by the generosity of the vicar and his

An early postcard of the interior of St Saviour's Church. It is addressed to Miss H. Shepherd, I. or T.C.A, Nr Hitchin and date-stamped '07. The message reads "D.H. How do you like this would like to see you there. With love from H.W.C"

family or by gifts and subscription from the congregation. Other enhancements were made on the occasion of the vicar's 70th birthday and the couple's golden wedding.

A memorial chapel was erected in 1934 at the East end of the North Aisle in memory of George Bernard Gainsford, the second vicar and son of the first. It was designed by W. Lawson of St Albans and the furnishings and fittings were mostly given by the Gainsford family. This chapel was dismantled in the early 1970's.

Holy Saviour's unusual claim to historical interest is not in its age as is true with many English churches, but in its foundation and patronage by the first vicar and his 45 years' incumbency and that of his son for a further 23 years, so that the first 68 years of the church's existence remained in the family. Their generosity extended beyond the church building and congregation, however. In addition, George Gainsford also founded an orphanage, schools and almshouses, still to be seen on the opposite side of the road, and a mission room at Walsworth, now St Faith's Church. The almshouses are still dwellings, although now called the Cloisters.

Holy Saviour started with practices considered very extreme towards the end of the 19th century; choral services, the choir dressed in surplices and chanting psalms and the service of Harvest Festival. In 1875, daily celebration of Holy Communion started, but regular communicants were ridiculed and persecuted, as Holy Communion in the Church of England was generally celebrated more infrequently.

The "High Church" tradition has continued at Holy Saviour; many of the practices considered 'very extreme' in 1865 are now common, but during Holy

The choir has always been strong at Holy Saviour Church. This picture from 1907 shows a large, but only male, choir. Nowadays the Church is graced with female voices, too. Older people from all over the town admit to having sung here as choirboys.
Back row: J H White, organist, B Day, H Watts, G Kirby, E P Seymour, E J Newell, F Cannon, W Pearmain, J Knight, J Prudence, W Palmer, W Winter, Graham, H R Watts, H Bloom.
Middle row: Foster, Proctor, Warrington, Rev G B Gainsford, Rev George Gainsford, Rev H H Maugham, Sayer, Blandford, Palmer.
Front row: G Lines, Angell, Lewis, F Marsom, Reed, H L Sayer, ???, F Denniss.
(Hitchin Museum.)

A stunning display! The Holy Saviour Church Christmas Tree Festival has been an annual event since 1997, lasting a whole weekend and attracting over 4,000 visitors at the last count! It averages around 50 trees on a wide variety of themes and the entries are divided into several categories. Local organisations, businesses and individuals engage in friendly competition and the resulting event raises large sums for church funds and selected charities. In 1998, the Festival achieved regional fame when the Church was visited by I.T.V.'s "About Anglia". David and Sheila Daw organised the event for the first ten years and have now passed it on to Brian and Pauline Caswell. (Photographer unknown, probably taken in 2001)

11th Hitchin Brownies enact "A Scene from the East" as their tableau for the annual Hitchin Hospital Carnival in 1932. Note the exotic raffia skirts and "enhanced" complexions! The late Margaret Richmond sits front right, wearing the large hooped ear rings. (Margaret Richmond)

Week in particular, services still have a different pattern in some ways from the rest of the Anglican churches in Hitchin and incense is still used on a regular basis.

Church organizations in the early days divided mostly into those of a devotional nature and those for practical help for the needy.

The devotional ones were demanding, requiring prayer, regular attendance and communion, giving of alms, no attendance at other denominations in England, charitable and evangelistic works and acting as a pressure group to Parliament on church matters.

Practical organizations included the Parish Lending Library, a Parish Nurse, Church Lads' Brigade, District Visitors, Clothing Club, St Saviour's Book Depot of religious literature, housed in Mr Marriott's shop on the corner of Radcliffe Road and Walsworth Road. A work guild provided clothes for the poor and old in the 1920s and a Girls' Aid Society raised funds for girls in trouble.

More social organizations began as time passed; Cubs (1934) and Scouts (1914), St Saviour's Church Players performed at Ascensiontide festivities (the Church's patronal festival) and at other times, no doubt. An over 21 club was formed for cultural activities in 1947 and a young wives' group founded by Mrs Nickisson, wife of the priest-in-charge of St Faith's in Walsworth, had a skiffle group. In 1923, the choirboys took the vicar for a drive in his motor in the country on Ascension Day; who was driving, we wonder? Things were definitely relaxing.

The biggest difference between then and now is church attendance. At the mission of 1875, there were between 90 and 100 communicants on the last day (the services were at 5.45 and 7.45 a.m!) On Easter Day there were 112 communicants at 7 a.m. and 136 at 8 a.m. On Sundays in 1912, the following services were held

Holy Eucharist	8 a.m. (Also at 7 a.m. last Sunday in the month
Infants' Service	10 a.m.
Matins	9.45 a.m. sung (1st in the month)
Eucharist with sermon	10.30 a.m.
Children's service	3 p.m.
Evensong & sermon	6.30 p.m.

In the mid 1880s, average attendance on Sunday evenings was 574. The 1871 census showed the population of Hitchin to be 8,850 and in the mid 1880s, places of worship in the town had seating capacity for 5,825 (comfortably!). Of course, there were no distractions like open shops and football matches on Sundays, not to mention television! In 1931, however, there were still 220 communicants on Easter Monday.

At a time when St Mary's had slums on the doorstep, the fashionable carriages were to be seen in Radcliffe Road, a sad reflection maybe on Christian priorities? The Churches of all denominations, however, provided the main welfare provision for the poor. All collections on Festival days were for charitable organizations.

Regular giving to the Church in the shape of pledges started as early as 1912, and continues to the present, enabling the Church to budget like any other organisation. Gone are the days of generous patrons.

Holy Saviour Church today still has a busy congregation, with a variety of social and devotional groups. In 1997 it was one of the first churches in the area to put on a Christmas Tree Festival which goes from strength to strength. The church has a beautiful interior, is well-known for its exceptionally good music and for being a welcoming and friendly place.

Vicars

Rev. George Gainsford, Founder	1865-1910
Rev. George Bernard Gainsford	1910-1933
Rev. Kenneth Wyche	1933-1940
Rev. Ernest Scott	1941-1949
Rev. C. Julian Cobern	1949-1965
Rev. Patrick Bright	1968-1975
Rev. Neil Steadman	1976-1984
Rev. David Hall	1985-1992
Rev. Frank Mercurio	1993-2000
Rev. Jane Fox	2001-2008
Rev. Ian Todd	2009-

St Saviour's Almshouses (The Cloisters)

A trust deed for almshouses and orphanage dated 14th August 1869 was signed in the presence of Edward Marriott and T.H. Chance and enrolled in Her Majesty's High Court of Chancery, 26th August 1869. Both foundations had to be built within seven years or the monies and property would be used for other pious and charitable purposes connected with the Church of England at the discretion of the trustees. There were to be no more than six and no fewer than two trustees, all of whom had to be communicant members of the Church of England. The first trustees appointed were the Reverend George Gainsford, Thomas Alexander Dashwood, Charles Willes Wilshere, John Gurney Hawkins, Richard Henry

A present day photograph of the interior of The Cloisters, backed by the bell-tower of Holy Saviour Church. The room over the porch was designated as the Vicar's Room, a name which still continues. We don't know what its purpose was in the beginning, but in recent times, it has been used for church committee meetings and a Sunday School class. Home Start- North Hertfordshire began in this room in the 1980s and only vacated it recently. (Ashley Walker)

Pedder and the Reverend James Benjamin Parker. Their first meeting took place on 19th February 1870 by which time there were sufficient funds to start building. Plans for six almshouses were considered; George Gainsford paid for Nos 1 to 4 from funds, Mr Wilshere paid for No 5 and Mr Parkins for No 6. This entitled them to appoint the residents subject to the approval of the trustees. The plans were approved, and the tender by local builder, George Warren for £550 was accepted on October 10th 1870. The final account, passed on 30th December 1870, was for £574. Rent was charged to the Reverend George Gainsford for garden ground adjacent to the almshouses.

In the first few years, the trustees seemed to meet only for specific reasons, mostly to appoint new residents.

Another almshouse, No 7, was built in 1881 at Mr Hawkins' expense and in 1890, another two, Nos 8 and 9, were built by the Reverend George Gainsford, plus a house, No 10, for the Parish Nurse. A room over the gateway was also constructed and is named the 'Vicar's Room' to this day.

In 1896, sash windows for lead and iron casements in the six front houses were paid for by a twenty guinea legacy from the Reverend Parker, curate in the Holy Saviour Parish 1867-71, who died in 1892. The free standing house on the left of the courtyard facing the original chapel of the orphanage and numbered twelve, was built in 1910 in memory of Mrs Gainsford. In 1911, the Reverend George Bernard Gainsford assumed chairmanship of the trustees after the death of his father, the Reverend George Gainsford.

Over the years, there were numerous trustees appointed, many of whom are familiar names in Hitchin, such as W. Tindall Lucas, William Onslow Times, prominent in Hitchin as a local councillor, Ernest Bowman, the miller, J. Ransom and G. Hill. In 1919, Mr James Knight, the builder, was thanked for his improvement to the sanitary arrangements which were undertaken as a thanksgiving for the cessation of hostilities at the end of the First World War.

A curious design of chimney pot in the Cloisters.

A plaque commemorating the benevolence of John Gurney Hawkins, Hitchin solicitor and one of the original Trustees.

For the residents in the early days of The Cloisters, there were fairly stringent conditions and regulations. They were to be poor and deserving, either single, married or widowed communicants of the Church of England and at least sixty years old. Trustees could remove residents if they acquired property, were absent for more than one month in any one year without permission, for neglecting their religious duties, immoral or disorderly conduct, refusing to abide by the rules, allowing others to reside there or damaging property.

The following story of a man returning to the road of his birth, shows The Cloisters as a good place to retire to in the middle of the 20th Century, the availability of public houses being a special attraction!

Little Francis John ("Frank") Wells was born in Radcliffe Road in 1874, the son of a bricklayer. He was a musical boy and sang in St. Saviour's Church choir. He followed his father into the building trade and eventually became a Master Builder, setting-up his business in West Hill. In 1897, he "obliged" by filling-in as organist at Langley Parish Church, a post which lasted for 61 years! He claimed to have worn out two American organs and two bicycles during his tenure

By the early-1950s, Frank Wells was thinking of retirement and came to live at No 6, The Cloisters. He had been a widower for many years, and was adept at looking after himself. His day began with a trip down to "St. Luke's" in Walsworth Road, where he stoked the boilers for the little private school. The two ladies who ran it were fond of him, and saw that he didn't go hungry! His next stop was "The Radcliffe Arms", where he fortified himself with a pint of Bitter. Frank's granddaughter, Pansy Mitchell (*née* Wells), used to visit him at home in the afternoons, where he would invariably be sitting close to his little cast-iron fireplace, in the "special chair" presented to him on his retirement by the grateful parishioners of Langley. A feature of the room was the imposing "Butler's sink". Time also had to be found for tending his "Cloisters'" plot.

The last duty of the day was a gentle stroll to the nearby "Gloucester Arms" for an evening "pint". He remained healthy and active almost to the end, dying at the ripe old age of 89, in 1962.

Frank Wells in The Cloisters in 1957
(Hitchin Museum)

The Cloisters still has elderly residents, but their lives are no longer dictated by rules and they do not have to be churchgoers. The buildings have not been altered much although the chapel which accompanied the orphanage was converted into two flats; the upper one was inhabited for a number of years by Elizabeth York. Elizabeth had been in service with the Gilbertson family, well-known doctors in Hitchin and friends of the Gainsfords. She was Sacristan at Holy Saviour Church for many years and was meticulous in her duties, no doubt learned from her upbringing in St Margaret's Convent in Sussex, where her godmother was the Mother Superior. Her flat was equally neat and pleasing and she dispensed tea and coffee with doilies and tray cloths and made visitors feel very cosseted.

St Saviour's Orphanage (St Bridget's)

The trust deed of 14th August 1869 for the almshouses also provided for the building of an orphanage next door, now known as St Bridget's. Three roods of land were conveyed to the trustees for the two buildings and grounds. It was intended for twelve girls whose fathers had died or deserted them. Subscriptions for the building started in April 1869 and according to a newspaper report of 1873 when the building opened, approximately £340 had been collected. It was estimated that the building would cost about £460 with an additional £150 for furniture, so that there was still a sum of about £272 to be found. The same report describes the architecture as "somewhat ecclesiastical in its style, carried out in red brick with ornamental string courses, and forming a pleasant contrast to the surrounding houses. George Gainsford had designed it himself and it was thoroughly suitable to the purpose for which it was designed. The lower part of the Orphanage contains the children's day room, Sister's room, entrance hall, kitchen and offices; and on the upper floor are the children's dormitory and two other bedrooms."

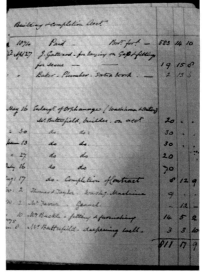

Orphanage Building Account 1873. Holy Saviour Church District Church Council Document (Hertfordshire Archives & Local Studies)

It was opened by and received the benediction of the Bishop of Rochester on 15th June 1873. It was enlarged in 1874 by the addition of an oratory and a wash-house and a chapel was added in 1875. By this time twenty seven children were resident. Sister Elisabeth from St Margaret's Convent in East Grinstead, Sussex, was appointed from the beginning, and is lovingly remembered still for her wonderful needlework in the Church. The best gold altar frontal was embroidered by her and is still used for the high festivals of the church year.

Over the years funds were raised in various ways for improvements. By 1913, there were two sisters from St Margaret's looking after twenty four girls, aged 4 to 16. At the beginning a weekly charge of five shillings was made, presumably paid by a mother or other relative. For this, the girls were clothed, fed and educated and would eventually be employed in service or some other position. They wore blue dresses and pinafores and heavy red-lined cloaks in winter and had uniform haircuts. Their religious training was 'carefully attended to'; they all had to attend Church of England services regularly and exclusively and could be dismissed for disobedience or gross misconduct.

In 1933, the Orphanage closed and stood empty for some months. It was then taken over by a trust founded by the vicar, Father Kenneth Wyche, and run in conjunction with Holy Family Homes, administered by a central church society at Church House in Westminster. It was called St Saviour's Home for Girls and soon became known as St Bridget's.

A photograph of the children and staff taken in the Orphanage Garden in the Summer of 1886. The little girls in the front row are proudly displaying their dolls, although one appears to have been discarded! Two older ones are either knitting or darning. The 21 children are accompanied here by four members of staff and the children have been immaculately 'groomed' for the photograph. The term "inmates" could reflect Society's attitude at the time or the term may not have had the pejorative meaning of today. (Lawson Thompson Scrapbooks, Hitchin Museum)

Rear of the Chapel, now part of The Cloisters, from the back garden of St Bridget's , seen on the left of the picture. The small bell turret on the Chapel has long since disappeared. (Rev. Jane Fox)

Decreasing numbers led to the closure of the Home in 1955. It was offered to the Urban District Council as a house for the elderly, but there is no evidence that the offer was accepted and the building was empty for some time. Shortly after the Second World War, the Ministry of Health regulations required certain alterations to be made, such as lowered ceilings, which brought the Home into debt, so the building was sold to pay it off. By this time, it was not in the best state of repair as radiators had been installed and a severe winter caused the boilers to burst while the house was empty. It had also been occupied by vagrants. It was bought by John Myatt from the Trustees in 1957. He remembers a small room on the ground floor, divided in two, one half of which housed a very large boiler, and one of the windows had been used as a coal chute!

All of the girls went to St Saviour's School except for a few in later years who went on at secondary level to Hitchin Girls' Grammar School or Hitchin High School for Girls, (now The Priory School).

A picture of life in the Orphanage has been gathered from various sources.

Sylvia Spencer, niece of the artist Stanley Spencer, wrote an autobiography, published in 1997. She had been left at St Margaret's Convent, East Grinstead at the age of three and moved around between the Convent, her mother and foster parents throughout her childhood. (Children counted as orphans if their father was deceased or had deserted the family). She spent a few months at the Orphanage in Hitchin and was obviously very happy there, as the following extracts show.

"The orphanage at Hitchen (*sic*) was run by two loving nuns for a handful of children, in a house opposite the church. I immediately forgot about my parents in the happiness of belonging where there was nothing to be afraid of. The back of the house led on to a small playground, where the games, during this summer term, were all new to me; hoops and tops that you whacked to keep them spinning, different kinds of skipping, and best of all, hopscotch, which fascinated me so much, I could hardly wait to get into the playground to play another game.

Sometimes the nuns would bring some soapy water out, and in great contentment we would vie with each other to see who could blow the biggest and most colourful bubbles.

'Look at mine … look at mine then!'

Mealtimes held no fears for me here, and when cabbage was cooked, they would bring out the water it was cooked in for us to drink. I didn't like it much, but they said it would do us good, and were so pleased with us for drinking it, that I grew to love it for what it stood for. I can still see their short, well-clothed shapes, and feel their loving kindness as they moved towards us with the trayed cabbage water.

At the adjacent village (*sic*) school, I was aware of being special … we were watched over by our parents …the two nuns next door. When we went to church, we also felt special, dressed in old, soft blue nurses' cloaks lined in bright red.

Walks were often adventurous. There was the day when we ran about in a field and clambered over an old straw stack with shouts of delight, disappointed when we at last had to go home. But when it rained, the little sitting room was cosy. Sometimes we did sewing and mending, but often played snakes and ladders. Such was their love of us, I felt they liked us to be home, coming into the room to see what we were up to, and enjoying our happiness…

The intuitive, homely sisters of St Saviour's were able to convey affection as well as security. As a child I knew the difference…

Some years ago I went back to Hitchen (*sic*) and found that St Saviour's Orphanage, where I had been so happy had become an almshouse. There I met Miss York, a very old lady who went to St Margaret's Orphanage in 1908, and left some years before my arrival."

In the late 1960s, the chapel of St Bridget's was converted into two flats and it became part of the Cloisters, but before that, it stood empty for some years and a scout member of the Church remembers the scouts drying out their tents inside after camping.

Patsy Myatt, until recently the occupant of the top flat at St Bridget's was told years ago that in fine weather a parrot was put outside St Bridget's on a stand. This parrot is mentioned in Cherie Barras's reminiscence as being called Laura. Patsy has also had contact with other previous residents of St Bridget's.

Alice Dole, Louisa Ashbee and Dorothy Raiment, all sisters (*née* Martin), have all visited St Bridget's in recent years and Louisa with her husband, John and son, also John, returned on April 6th 2010. While going round St Bridget's she remembered all the rooms accurately, as shown in the plan *(next page)*. They remembered their mother used to visit sometimes and always at Christmas and Easter. Louisa recollects that she came to live at St Bridget's in 1935 and left in 1944 at the age of 16. She says "My earliest recollection was that the home was run by Nuns in my early years and then changed to a Matron and assistant Matron, it was a very strict upbringing, with the older girls looking after the younger ones, there was very little time for play, but I suppose it probably wasn't much different from what took place in ordinary homes that had large families. One of my chores at a very young age was to get up early

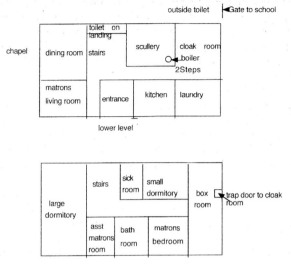

```
                    outside toilet  |◄Gate to school
   ┌──────────────────────────────────────────────┐
   │          │ toilet on │                        │
   │          │ landing   │ scullery │ cloak  room │
   │ chapel   │ dining room│ stairs  │             │
   │          │            │         │  ○─boiler   │
   │          │            │         │   2Steps    │
   │          ├────────────┼─────────┼─────────────┤
   │          │ matrons    │         │             │
   │          │ living room│ entrance│ kitchen │laundry│
   └──────────────────────────────────────────────┘
                    lower level
```

```
   ┌──────────────────────────────────────────────┐
   │          │        │ sick │ small     │        │
   │          │ stairs │ room │ dormitory │ box    │ ►trap door to cloak
   │ large    │        │      │           │ room   │  room
   │ dormitory├────────┼──────┼───────────┤        │
   │          │ asst   │ bath │ matrons   │        │
   │          │ matrons│ room │ bedroom   │        │
   │          │ room   │      │           │        │
   └──────────────────────────────────────────────┘
                    upper level
```

Plan drawn by Louisa Ashbee (nee Martin) from memory. When someone was in the sick room, a sheet was hung over the door to prevent infection spreading. The large dormitory held 20 beds and was for the younger girls. When John and Patsy Myatt moved into St Bridget's the marks of the iron bedsteads were still visible on the floor. The small dormitory was for older girls, but there was only the one bathroom for all including staff. The spy hole between the Assistant Matron's Room and the large dormitory is still visible.

and light the boiler, the boiler was known to us as "Jumbo". Apparently they washed their own sheets and didn't have much in the way of treats, no toys or presents, but they had parties at Christmas and a visit to the pantomime on Boxing Day and every summer went on holiday to St Michael's Mount in Cornwall where "a rich man took us out in his yacht"

Cynthia Stokes (*née* Wills) was at St Bridget's in the early 1940s and attended Hitchin Girls' Grammar School in 1947. She re-visited Hitchin in 1993 and knew Cherie Barras (*née* MacGuire), one of Cyndy's 'little ones'. Cherie was at St Bridget's from 1945, aged two, until 1955, one of the longest residents. Cherie Barras died in 1999, but in 1997 she wrote a detailed account of her time there, including a description of the layout of the house.

Louisa Ashbee and her late sister, Dorothy, in the foreground, on a nostalgic visit to St Bridget's in 2004. They were two of three sisters who had lived there when it was a Children's Home. (Louisa Ashbee)

St Bridget's residents in the 1940s. The Reverend Ernest Scott, Vicar of Holy Saviour Church is second left on the back row. Louisa Ashbee, née Martin, is standing second left middle row and her sister Dorothy is in the middle with the Archdeacon's hand on her shoulder. On his right is "Auntie Mate" (short for Matron), the Assistant Matron. Back row second right is Molly Tizard and front right, in the checked dress, is Frances Newell whose grandmother lived in the Cloisters. In later life, she was a lecturer and on one occasion talked about being brought up in an orphanage. This lecture took place in a Church where Louisa's sister-in-law attended and Louisa and Frances were reunited as a result and organized a reunion with some of the other girls. (Louisa Ashbee)

"All the matrons were called Auntie. Looking back it was a cosy world when Auntie Margaret and Auntie Mate (short for "Matron") were in charge". She describes little straw hats with silk flowers around the brim that they wore to church at Easter, Mothering Sunday when the Church gave all the children small posies of violets, to take back to the home, Harvest Festival when the church always donated the food to St Bridget's and how they sometimes dared one another to sneak down in the night and take the apples from the cupboard and have a midnight feast.

Auntie Margaret bought Cherie's first doll and made clothes for it. "Because this was the only doll I had it was very important to me". Birthdays were made special with presents of toys donated by other girls and a choice of treats such as a visit to the open air swimming pool. There was a birthday cake and a school friend was allowed to come

Footscraper at St Bridget's front door.

for tea. Christmas was enjoyed much as in any family according to her account. Most of the girls seemed to have visitors at some point, but she talks of this being unsettling. Some of them had a small plot of the garden to tend. But it wasn't all fun!

"Chores, there were always chores, every girl had to do cleaning, peeling potatoes, darning socks, making beds the list was endless" and she remembers one matron as being very harsh. When the home was being refurbished the girls were farmed out to different people and Cherie went to 'Auntie Holloway' who lived opposite. She was very kind and continued to take an interest in her after the home was finished and they moved back. Jill Higginson who now lives next to the Church also remembers Auntie Maud Holloway who "lived at No 53 Radcliffe Road, made lovely treacle toffees which she used to sell... Mrs Smith of No 55 Radcliffe Road, adopted a young girl from

The back of St Bridget's from the Vicarage garden (St Aidan's in Verulam Road), drawn by the Reverend Patrick Bright in the 1970s. (Patsy Myatt)

St Bridget's. St Bridget's had a television and a party was held there for the Coronation in 1953."

Florence A. McRobert, aged 86 in 2001 sent an extract from her autobiography. Her mother, Lily Greening was at St Bridget's and had her fees paid by a daughter of St Saviour's Church vicar. As Lily lived from 1885-1952 it would have been one George Gainsford's five daughters. She was happy there and remembered Sister Catherine and Sister Agnes were making an altar frontal for the church, but Sister Agnes died before it was completed. Lily Greening used to hold the threads for her.

Although St Bridget's is no longer a home for girls, the building has the same appearance from the exterior and at the time of going to print, it is still in the possession of John Myatt after more than fifty years.

St Saviour's School (Gainsford Court)

In 1867, it was planned to build a small school room and a notice to this effect was posted on Holy Saviour Church door on 30th June. The school was to be for both sexes, as self-supporting as possible and not under government control. The Vicar and churchwardens were to be trustees and managers. £200 was estimated for the cost of the building with the addition of a teacher's cottage at a later date. The site and a donation of £20 were given by George Gainsford and other gifts included £30 from Trinity College, Cambridge. By 23rd March 1869, £295.13.3 had been raised. Building work was by William Butterfield of Hitchin from a design by the Reverend George Gainsford

St Saviour's School 1918. Rene Parsell, Jill Spooner's mother is 4th from the left in the second row back. (Jill Spooner)

The Sunday school and day school opened in 1868 and the fund for the Mistress's cottage started. The sum of £146.12.11 was raised by the end of 1870 and the cottage was also built by William Butterfield. Mrs Gent and a monitor were paid £5.12.6 per quarter year and J. Buckle was paid 4s.8d.per quarter for cleaning and sundries. Total expenditure for 1868 was £41.5.0.

St Saviour's School Badge in the 1940s

In 1870 a fund was set up for enlarging the school room. From 1870 the Mistress's salary was fixed at 9s per week with the rent-free cottage. The monitor received £1.5.0 per quarter. In 1874, funds of £117.15.1 were raised for a new classroom. The school was placed under government inspection in 1873. Another new school room was added in 1910.

At the Annual Parochial Meeting in 1931, the Vicar said he deplored "authority's" wish to send all senior girls to other schools in the town, as parents did not want older girls to be taught by men.

A number of well-attended school reunions have been held recently in Holy Saviour Church Hall. These have produced a lot of memories which paint a wonderful picture of school life from about the 1920s to the 1950s. The school must have had a good reputation in the 1940s as four pupils travelled by bus from Whitwell every day. In the 1930s, everyone went home for dinner midday, but by the 1940s, dinner was being served in St Anne's Hall in Garden Row which was just as well for the Whitwell four!

We have descriptions of the interior layout of the school, the pot-bellied coke stove, the subjects taught, differing attitudes to obligatory church-going and life at the school during the 1939-45 war as illustrated by the following first-hand accounts.

Sisters, **Nancy Mattausch** and **Olive Van Klaveren** remember their time at the school.

"When I started at the school in 1936 we learned to write our first letters and numbers on slates with very squeaky slate pencils...When we went into the juniors at about 7, we had to learn to do joined-up writing with a steel-nibbed pen which you dipped in ink. Every desk had an inkwell which had to be re-filled from big stone jars. When you were writing it was very hard not to make blots. Some teachers used to rap you on the knuckles for messy work...We used to do P.T. (physical training) in the playground a few times a week. A lot of it was Swedish drill, i.e. standing in lines doing arm and leg exercises.

We also did country dancing (some of the boys in hob-nailed boots!), maypole dancing and a game called stoolball, where teams took turns in hitting a ball against a wooden board on a post. In needlework lessons (in the lower juniors) we used to make felt pen-wipers and needle-cases and milk-jug covers....

When the war started, we were all fitted with gas masks. We had to wear them in class for one lesson every day to get used to them. We had to take them with us wherever we went. They were in brown cardboard boxes, with a long string to carry them over your shoulder. Later you could buy more fancy carriers, in different shapes, materials and colours.

About the same time, identity cards were introduced. Everyone had a card with a number and you had to memorise your number; mine was DEJQ 202 4.

St Saviour's School 1923 *(Jane Eddy)*
Back Row: *2nd right: Rene Parsell, Jill Spooner's mother* Middle Row: *Far right: teacher, Miss Moundsman* Front Row: *?, Winifred Anderson, Eva Cook, Gladys Cook, ?, ?   , ?*

St Saviour's School Class 4 1930s. *(Mary Bradbeer)*
Back Row:*Muriel Dorrington, Betty Matthews, Mary Else, Joy Watts, Eileen Nottage, Daisy Alderman, Phyllis Austin.* 2nd Row:*Jean Jenkins, Jean Smith, Barbara Hillier, Beryl Allen, Dorothy Goldsmith, Minnie Walker, Phyllis Sayer, Mary Upchurch.* 3rd Row: *Alma Kirby, ? ,Winnie Minnis, Barbara Foster, Eileen Gilbert, Doris Albone, Winnie Bullock, Kathleen Mansell, Patricia Timoney, Marie Wootton.* 4th Row: *Geoffrey Hubbard, Douglas Smith, ? , Walter Smith, ?, Bobby Hoy*

Our school became very crowded at this time because evacuee children had to use the building too; although we were only 35 miles north of London, we had two girls from Stepney in the East End. I remember the day they came – a large group of boys and girls walking from the station, each with a luggage label pinned to his or her coat and holding brown paper carrier bags with a few clothes, a tin of condensed milk, a large block of chocolate and half-a-crown…..

The winter of 1941-2, when I was in my last year at junior school, was a very cold one. A lot of snow fell, some of which was still around in March. Fuel was in short supply and we had to wear coats, gloves and hats (balaclava helmets or 'pixie hoods'– all knitted) in school. The classrooms just had a coke stove in each to heat them (very smelly fumes often came from them). There were 48 children in the class and we used to have marks for practically everything we did."

Mary Bradbeer (*née* Upchurch) has the following memories.

"I started at St Saviour's School in 1929 when I was 5 years old…I remember the bottles of milk being delivered each morning from Alderman's Dairy (in Walsworth Road): in winter they were placed round the stove.

The pupils in the school were divided into houses named after authors or poets, blue badge for Shakespeare, green for Dickens, yellow for Longfellow and red for Wordsworth. I was in Dickens team… One other memory – we never referred to the lavatory by name, we had to say 'please may I go to the court?' When the boat race came round a man would often stand outside the school selling celluloid dolls dressed in light or dark blue feathers. Other times a man with a horse and cart would be outside the school at dinner time, handing out leaflets asking for bags of old clothes; if we took some back after dinner we would receive a toy.

Regarding the church, we went to services every Friday during Lent and also Ascension Day.

One day the school was invited to Rev. Gainsford's house 'Woodside' – in what is now Woodside car park – to see Queen Mary's doll house. Later vicars were Father Wyche, who would come into the school with his pet marmoset on his shoulder, then Father Reader who also was at St Faith's and Father Mason (curates) who spoke so quickly the services he took were finished much quicker.

St Saviour's always took part in the singing festivals and won quite a few times. At Christmas a concert for parents was held in St Anne's Hall in Garden Row.

I must say here that I think Mrs Smith was an excellent headmistress, always approachable and helpful to the children. I can never remembering her losing her temper."

Margaret Gibbs, (*née* Marshall) was a pupil in the 1930s.

"I started at St Saviour's School in 1936, my earliest memory is of a large classroom divided by a rather inadequate curtain. There was a class of about forty children on either side of this curtain and the two teachers had to try to teach two groups of five and six year olds at the same time…

Another memory was of being taken into the Church, I don't think it was every week, perhaps on festival days or special occasions. My class, which was the youngest, would file out of the classroom and a class of older children would take each one of us by the hand and lead us across the road into the Church. I remember being most impressed (as I still am) by the beauty and atmosphere inside. Once my minder dipped her finger in the Holy Water and touched my forehead and it made me feel very 'good', but I don't think it lasted long!"

The following passage from **Audrey Foster,** (*née* White), shows how different attitudes to church-going can be, even among children.

"I attended St Saviour's School as a pupil from 1932-38. Mrs Smith was the head teacher...I went back to St Saviour's School as a qualified teacher from Easter 1948 until September 1950. I taught the middle infant class in the large room in the infant block. I shared the room with the top infant class. The room was divided only by a short curtain, the children could look under it and teachers could look over the top! The children were still writing on slates. The uncovered toilets were outside in the yard, very unpleasant when it was raining! Mrs Smith was still the head teacher...

Another vivid memory was of attending St Saviour's Church on Ascension Day. I was brought up a Baptist so was mystified by the swinging of incense which made me feel very sick. When I went back as a member of staff I volunteered to take out any children who felt unwell – a good excuse for me to leave the service! The best part of the day was that after the service we had the rest of the day as a holiday."

Pauline Rowland, almost a decade later has vivid memories, too.

"I started at St Saviour's School at the age of 4 years in 1942 and stayed until 1949....Another memory was of Father Scott; the garden to the rectory (*sic*) opened onto the playground and whenever he walked across the playground to the church, this rather rotund figure all in black would be surrounded by children (rather like the pied piper). We had our school dinners in St Anne's Hall, again all queuing to enter and it seemed to have a smell all of its own, obviously the cooking aromas but the building as well. When you moved from infants to juniors you used a different playground; this contained the outside toilets. I can see the green wooden doors now (I do not ever remember using them). The playground was grey tiled and either had tall brick walls or iron railings, while the infant one was tarmac."

Lesley Bacon, the last of our school contributors, remembers the teachers and the orphans particularly.

"I attended St Saviour's School for two years 1949-1951. The first classroom I was in was downstairs. It had a coal fire and wooden desks which accommodated two pupils per desk. There was a wooden folding partition which separated us from the next class. This could be folded back when we had morning assembly. We had a teacher called Mr Foster who could become very irate and would throw chalk or the blackboard duster at the boys...

The girls who lived at St Bridget's (the orphanage) also attended the school. They were occasionally allowed a friend to visit them for tea. I was surprised that they had to stand behind their chairs until the prayer had been said. Some of the girls had relations but were unable to live with them. My parents invited them to our house in Verulam Road for a Christmas party. A girl called Eileen Fennick said it was just like Downing Street. We never discovered why Downing Street."

Teachers

Most of the ex-pupils remembered the names of their first teachers and who was liked or not! Miss Hall is mentioned more than once as being exceptionally kind to the new children. Miss or Mrs Smith who was headmistress in the 1930s and 1940s is also mentioned by many as very popular. The following dates are approximate and taken from the accounts written by the ex-pupils. Many teachers stayed a long time, so the school must have had good continuity.

Lesley Carlisle*	1916 & 1917
Agnes Hillman*	1917
Louisa Allen*	1910 or 1917
Victoria Primett*	1917
Miss Rainbird (governess?)	1918-24 approx
Miss Russell (married one of the Hawkins)	1920s?
Eileen Moore*	1923
Mrs Dowling	1930s to 1940s
Mrs Downing	1920s
Miss or Mrs Davis	1940s
Miss Moundsman	1920s
Miss Surridge (Head)	1918-24 approx.
Mrs Spicer	1918-24 approx.
Mrs Bannister	1918-24 approx.
Mrs Howard	1918-24 approx.
Miss or Mrs Hall (First class)	1920s to 1940s
Mrs Sophie Smith (Head)	1920s to late 1940s
Miss D.M. Baxter	1920s to 1930s
Miss Stock	late 1920s to 1930s
Miss Johnson	late 1920s to 1940s
Miss Baxter	1930s
Miss Harrington	1930s
Miss Cooper	1930s
Miss Fielding	1930s
Miss Cookson (Mrs Smith's niece)	1930s to 1940s
Miss Browning	1930s
Mr & Mrs Milner (he later became Head)	1940s to 1950s
Miss Fisher	1930s to 1940s
Mr Foster	later 1940s early 1950s
Mrs Audrey Foster (*née* White)	1948-50

Old girls of Hitchin Girls' Grammar School

St Saviour's School closed in 1954 and a thanksgiving mass was held on 21st December for the work of the school. In 1955, St Andrew's Infant and Junior School, the joint responsibility of St Saviour's and St Mary's, opened in the old St Mary's School building in Churchyard until the new school was ready in Benslow Lane, its present site. In 1956, the St Saviour's School building re-opened, refurbished as the Gainsford Memorial Hall in memory of the first two vicars, and it served as the church hall until 1977 when it was sold to the Sikh community for their Gurdwara. The Sikhs moved out in 2006, having constructed a purpose-built Gurdwara elsewhere in the town, and the building has now been converted sensitively to dwellings and named Gainsford Court. The façade has been retained, the brickwork cleaned and re-pointed and various features have

Standing in front of the beautifully converted St Saviour's School building , now Gainsford Court, are, left to right, Jane and Nicholas Gainsford (great grandson of the Reverend George Gainsford) and Rosemary Gainsford, widow of Nicholas's brother, David.
The bottom picture shows the information plaque placed by the Hitchin Historical Society in April 2009.

been improved in keeping with the period of the building, such as replacing inappropriate windows and placing decorative ridge tiles on the roof to match the almshouses and orphanage next door.

This conversion was recognized by being granted the Civic Award for 2008 by the Hitchin Society at its Annual General Meeting on 16th March 2009. A commemorative plaque was mounted on the front of the building by the Hitchin Historical Society and on 3rd April 2009 was unveiled by Nicholas Gainsford, great-grandson of the founder of the school and his sister-in-law, Rosemary. Nicholas's wife, Jane gave a short speech of thanks for those who keep the family name alive.

MISS WARR begs to inform her patrons and friends that she has REMOVED her School, from Bucklersbury to No. 1, RADCLIFFE ROAD.
Hitchin Station, Feb. 19, 1869.

No 1 Radcliffe Road

The advertisement illustrated is the only clue to the occupant of this address in the late 1860s, but who was Miss Warr? What was her Christian name and the name of her school? There is no indication of what she may have taught at her school; could it have been music, art or even a sewing class? Unfortunately Miss Warr seems to be untraceable as no records have been found, although a Warr family is mentioned in the 1861 census as living at Northern Railway Cottages. A daughter named Mary was 11 at that time, so in 1869, she would have been 19 and could conceivably have been advertising as a teacher. There are no Warrs recorded in the 1871 census, however. Could someone's family tree provide the answers? This is one of many mysteries that have gone unsolved in the Triangle area for over a hundred years.

A little later, however, another occupant of this address is rather better documented. John King was born in Campton, Bedfordshire in 1843 to parents John and Sarah King. In 1861, John, aged eighteen was living at 14 Holme Street, Bedford and described as a journeyman tailor. In 1870, John married Elizabeth Gaylor of Hitchin and they lived together with Elizabeth's widowed mother at 4 Whinbush Grove, Whinbush Road, Hitchin. By 1878 they had moved to 1 Radcliffe Road and in 1901 John was still in the tailoring business. John and

---

JOHN KING,

PRACTICAL + TAILOR,

RADCLIFFE ROAD, HITCHIN.

Those who want good value for money should try J. KING, for

Overcoats from 28/-, Suits from 42/-, Trousers from 10/6.

ONE SHILLING IN THE POUND DISCOUNT FOR CASH.

Elizabeth lived at this address for over thirty years, Elizabeth dying in 1914, aged seventy six and John in 1927, aged eighty seven. They are both buried in Hitchin Cemetery.

There are many and varied architectural details in this road, such as chimney pots and chimney stacks of different designs, Victorian footscrapers and decorative cast-iron drain covers, some of which are shown throughout the book.

So many Victorian buildings in one narrow road has brought its problems, however, because of increasing traffic. A dearth of garages meant a lot of on-street parking by residents and, on Sundays, by the congregations of Holy Saviour Church and the Gurdwara. Congestion worsened with the introduction of "pinch-points" in the 1980s, which eased somewhat when a one-way system came into force later. Now that there is a residents' parking scheme, it is hoped that this has been solved to a certain extent.

A moment in time captured in a tranquil Radcliffe Road a century ago. The railings, long since removed, probably for the war effort in the 1940s, give a very neat and tidy appearance to the road, but the façades of the houses are still recognisable. A dapper delivery man halts his cart near the crown of the road, while the pedestrians pose for what must have been a rare photographic opportunity. The Church of the Holy Saviour is clearly visible on the right of the picture. (Hitchin Museum)

This side passage to 1 Radcliffe Road (left) *has a curious series of arches, the outer one being a rounded Norman arch and the internal ones in the pointed Gothic style. Is there a structural reason for this or is it merely a decorative feature?*

Chapter 5

Dacre Road

Dacre Road was formed from the same plot of land as Radcliffe Road and took its name from Sir Thomas Brand, Lord Dacre who was a Member of Parliament for Hertfordshire at the time.

Many of the houses were built during the 1860s for the expanding workforce drawn by the arrival of the railway. Larger houses were occupied by families with a servant.

"Royal" Dacre Road!

Unlikely as it may seem, the Triangle has a very real "royal connection"!

Turn into the road from Nightingale Road, and look to your left. One of the houses, No 58, once "Lopside", is an imposing and solidly-built presence, slightly out-of-scale with its smaller neighbours. Today, after a period of neglect, it is used as social housing, but its earlier history is intriguing.

In the early 1880s, Andrew Wilkie, a prosperous cabinet maker and upholsterer, brought his wife and six children from London to Hitchin. Their previous home

View of Holy Saviour Church overlooking Dacre Road. Drawn for a Christmas card by the Reverend Patrick Bright, 1970. (Patsy Myatt)

had been in Paddington, just off the Edgware Road, where Mr Wilkie had employed "a man, a woman and 6 boys" in his business. The family of six children soon grew to eight, which must have kept the Scots-born Mrs Elsie Wilkie very busy, as she managed the household with one young local live-in servant. The 1891 census lists their eldest child, "Elsie M." as a scholar. She was then 17 years old, demonstrating perhaps a family respect for the value of education. In many homes a daughter of that age would have been seen as a useful domestic addition.

By the time of the 1901 census, the young Elsie had "spread her wings". She now lived in Chertsey in Surrey, and was the "Assistant Schoolmistress" in a small private school run by the two Misses Coxworth. It is not known what drew her back to Hitchin, but "Lopside" was emptying of her younger siblings, and her father was now retired. She must certainly have been in possession of good references.

Miss Marion Wilkie, governess and teacher. (Bedfordshire & Hertfordshire Pictorial, July 1929)

The role of a governess was still a significant one in many upper- and middle-class families. Daughters and small sons were frequently taught at home, sometimes by a live-in tutor, but increasingly by a visiting one, now that modes of transport were improving. Sometimes a teacher would accept a few carefully chosen children into her own home, should it be suitable. Miss Wilkie did both in her time.

Certainly, by 1904, she was in the employ of the Bowes-Lyon family at St. Paul's Walden. The Countess of Strathmore initially engaged her to teach Lady Rose and the Hon. Michael on a daily basis, travelling in each day and taking lunch with the children. Later her pupils were the two youngest children, Lady Elizabeth and the Hon. David. A severe bout of double pneumonia put an end to this arrangement, as poor Miss Wilkie found the daily journey too taxing. The Countess of Strathmore then permitted the children to travel to Hitchin for some of their lessons, joining a carefully selected group in a schoolroom at "Lopside". Two of the children were the sons of the Reverend George Bernard Gainsford, Guy and Jasper, and there was a small girl whose parents lived in The Avenue.

A reporter from the "Bedfordshire and Hertfordshire Pictorial" interviewed Miss Wilkie's widowed mother in 1929, and recorded her memories of a small dark-haired "Betty" spending morning playtime in the "Lopside" kitchen, hoping that shortbread would appear, and of the little girl helping to pick the gooseberries in the back-garden.

No-one knows how long this arrangement lasted, presumably a wider curriculum would have been sought as she grew older, but Miss Wilkie was certainly connected to the Strathmore family for nine years. At the outbreak of the First World War the family dispersed, and the young Lady Elizabeth went to Glamis Castle with her mother. At some stage, Miss Wilkie, named "Elsie" like her mother, became "Marion" (her second initial was "M").

Following her brush with the nobility, Miss Wilkie continued to teach. No-one seems sure how long the select little group of children continued to learn in the "Lopside" schoolroom. There are unsubstantiated rumours that she "stepped into the breech" if a staffing emergency arose at St. Saviour's School. If so, it must have been quite a culture-shock! In 1918, she took up a temporary post to teach English and History to Junior Boys at Alleyne's Grammar School in Stevenage, and she remained there until her retirement in 1936. She was the first woman to be permanently appointed to their staff, and for many years the only one. She was much loved and respected. A tribute to her in a history of the school recalled "a small lady, proud of her Scots ancestry"…"who never made much of her royal connections". She donated a cricket prize, which is still awarded.

Miss Wilkie died in 1955, at the age of 81, following many years in nursing homes.

And what of "Lopside"? The Wilkie family vacated the house in the mid-1920s, when the widowed Mrs Wilkie and her daughter moved to Walsworth Road. Over the years, housing needs altered, and "Triangle" families no longer relished the upkeep of so large a property, however imposing. Eventually it was divided into flats, initially three, later two. In 1960, a young married couple moved to Hitchin from London, and the ground-floor flat became their first home.

The Harmers enjoyed the high ceilings and marble fireplaces, but probably not the lidded-bath in the kitchen, or the outside "loo". And certainly not "the lots and lots of spiders"! They had the use of the back garden, and a garage, and shared No 58 with two other households. The family's increasing size caused them to move on in 1964.

Over subsequent years, the once-proud address fell into a state of decay, not to say dereliction. It became the property of North Hertfordshire District Council, and escaped demolition by "a hair's breadth". Boarded-up windows and sprouting weeds did Dacre Road no credit. The past 35 years have seen the house's fortunes fluctuate, with periods of neglect causing anger and concern amongst its neighbours. Now, happily,

"Lopside" in 2009, a mid-nineteenth century, brick and tile house. Does its lack of symmetry give rise to its name?

"Lopside" is back in use as social housing, and serving the local community. As probably the most prestigious building in the whole of Dacre Road, one hopes that its value will be recognised both as a well-built and imposing property, but also as a link to its royal past!

Bill Harmer and baby Russel (1964) with De Havilland in the background. The spares department of De Havilland Aircraft Company was in Walsworth Road during the 1960s. (Margaret and Bill Harmer)

A fine stone carving detail (left) *on the frontage of 43/44 Dacre Road*

A view down Dacre Road from the junction with Walsworth Road, Summer 2005. Dominating the street scene is the red brick, mid-nineteenth century factory unit on the right. The attractive roof line further down the street provides a welcome contrast to the clogged kerbsides. (Ashley Walker)

Chapter 6

Verulam Road

Early records show that that this road was originally known as Green Lane and according to the 1844 map most of the land on both sides of it was owned by William Wilshere. The 1852 map shows at the very bottom of Green Lane a row of eight terraced cottages named 'Starlings Terrace', but these are long gone. By the 1860s, Green Lane was known as Nightingale Lane, a name which lasted until 1883 when the name of Verulam Road was adopted by the Local Board of Health at the request of the Reverend George Gainsford, Vicar of Holy Saviour Church in Radcliffe Road. Previously it had also been referred to as Love Lane, but as no records have been found to confirm this, it may only have been known as that by the people in the local area.

The land known as Great Whinbush Field in Green Lane and Whinbush Lane was purchased from William Wilshere around 1868 by Joseph Bennell, a Quaker farmer originally from Bedfordshire. In the early days, a large part of the road was taken up by The Grove, built by Joseph Bennell for his family home, later the Sacred Heart Convent and School; this estate stretched from Whinbush Road to Walsworth Road. Convent Close now stands on part of this site.

Joseph Bennell and The Grove

Joseph Bennell was born on 17th December 1798 in Houghton Conquest, Bedfordshire, the second son of Joseph and Mary Bennell. The family was involved in The Society of Friends in the Bedfordshire area throughout the eighteenth century and owned a considerable amount of land in Mid -Bedfordshire. Joseph arrived in Hitchin in the early 1830s with his wife, Elizabeth, and their three daughters, Jane, Maria and Lucy, but they did not stay long initially. A removal certificate issued by the Hitchin Monthly Meeting of the Society of Friends showed that they transferred to Mangrove, Albans Monthly Meeting of Friends on 25th November 1835. By 1845 the family had returned to Hitchin and were living in Bancroft Street. Joseph's wife, Elizabeth, died aged 66 in 1866 and is buried in the Friends' burial ground in Hitchin.

On the land Joseph had bought in 1868, he built a large Victorian House, called "The Grove", together with labourers' cottages, coach house and stables. He lived in "The Grove" with his daughter, Maria, Isabella Turner, a nurse and domestic servant and Sarah Tabraham, cook and domestic servant. Maria died, aged forty two, on 24th February 1874, (Jane, another daughter had died some years before) and Joseph continued to live at The Grove until his own death six years later on

TO LET, AT MICHAELMAS, A COTTAGE HOUSE, with four bedrc two good sized parlours, kitchen, scu cellar, coal house, &c., two w.cs.; also a Labo COTTAGE with either one or two bedrooms. are well supplied with water, and the gas is la Apply to J. BENNELL, The Grove, Hitchin.

One cottage was obviously comfortable with flush toilets and gas laid on, although there is no mention of WCs in the labourer's cottage! (Paternoster's Advertising File, 1863-1872. Hitchin Museum)

8th December 1880, aged eighty two. Both are buried in the Friends' Burial Ground in Hitchin.

Joseph made his last will a few days before he died. The house, cottages, coach house and stables were left to his only surviving daughter, Lucy and her husband, James Long whom she had married in 1858; James was from a wealthy Bedfordshire family of farmers and landowners. Joseph was meticulous in providing for the family, friends and servants. He bequeathed £100 to his nephew, Frederick Wright, and set up legacies for each grandchild for when they reached twenty one years of age. Any servant still in his employment at his death received a small sum and his house servant, William Merritt, received £15. His wearing apparel was shared between all of the labourers on his farm and his friend, Mrs Charlotte Shannon received ten guineas. By 1893, Lucy had put up part of the estate for sale.

It is uncertain when Lucy and James moved into the house, as James is recorded as dying in Henlow in 1890. Certainly by 1901, Lucy was living at "The Grove"

Residence of Joseph Bennell Hitchin

Sketch by an unknown artist of "The Grove", Joseph Bennell's residence, in the 1860s. (Lawson Thompson scrapbooks, Hitchin Museum)

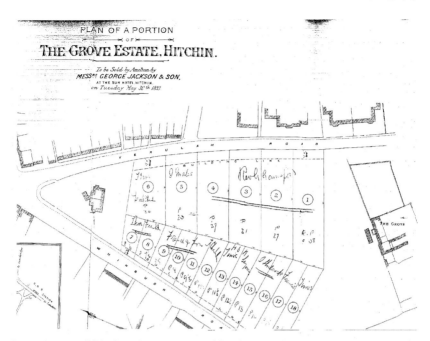

Lucy sold part of "The Grove" estate in 1893. This Auctioneer's plan shows that the house (to the right), surrendered much of its land to building development. Amongst the purchasers were well-known local names: Reverend G. Gainsford, J. Shilcock and French & Son (Builders) (Hitchin Museum)

with daughter, Amy Holden and two grandchildren, Arthur John and Olive Mary Holden and four servants. Lucy died on 23rd February 1905 at "The Grove" and probate was granted to her son, Arthur Long, D.S.O., an Army Major, and her daughter, Amy Holden.

The Grove passed out of the family in 1910 when it was sold to an American, Mr Sam T. Gresham. He then sold The Grove in 1922 and in 1924, the Sisters of the Sacred Heart Convent and School, at last found a more permanent home here after moving around the Triangle from one house to another.

A studio portrait of Joseph Bennell, owner of "The Grove", photographed in old age. (Hitchin Museum)

Sacred Heart Convent and School

The History of St Michael's College traces the Convent's 'progress' through the Triangle. Rose Cottage in Walsworth Road was the first home of the combined convent and school as mentioned in a previous chapter, although on first arriving in Hitchin, the nuns had been in York Road and then in Nos 15 and 16 Nightingale Road, where they ran a laundry in order to provide for themselves. With the lease running out on Rose Cottage in 1907 they needed a new home and moved into Nos 44 and 45 Walsworth Road opposite Rose Cottage, which they rented from the Horsfield family on a lease of seven years. Fees from the school were not sufficient for the upkeep of the establishment, so they took in lady boarders for whom "the best rooms were set aside". By 1914, they wanted to add a senior department to the school and as the present premises were too small, a new school building was erected at the rear of their cottages in Nightingale Road. Before the building was completed, an amusing incident occurred. Some Sisters from their Mother House in France were on the way to Canada but became stranded in Southampton because of the war, so made their way to the Hitchin home. "They arrived without warning, since the Sisters at Hitchin had no telephone, and were put in the dormitory of the new school. The building was not yet completed, and next morning a surprised workman unwittingly entered their room. It is not recorded who was the more embarrassed"

Sacred Heart Convent

DAY AND BOARDING SCHOOL

THE aim of the Sisters is to provide a thoroughly efficient modern education to the children confided to their care. Special attention is given to the formation of the will and heart of every individual pupil. The School stands in its own grounds and is only a few minutes from the Station and Town. Large class-rooms, library, music rooms, tennis lawns and large playing-field are special features.

THE INFANT DEPARTMENT
is taught on kindergarten lines

Directed by
THE SISTERS of THE SACRED HEART

HITCHIN

An advertisement in the Hitchin Official Guide of 1921; the details of the facilities and its location between town and station show the Sisters knew how to sell their school!

In 1921 there were seventy five day-pupils and fifteen boarders and numbers continued to increase, so a more spacious building with grounds for games was sought. The Sisters were not able to buy The Grove when it was first put up for sale by Lucy Bennell, but this time they were successful. They sold the school building in Nightingale Road and the equipment from the laundry which had closed in 1920 and were able to purchase The Grove and arrange for internal modification of the building. The school opened there in 1924 and "The boarders returned, two days before the day-pupils, to find central heating, hot and cold water in the dormitories, good playing space and tennis courts" This was luxury indeed in the mid-1920s!

All was not always what it seemed behind the walls of this decorous establishment, however. During the Second World War, there was, apparently, a lay teacher at the Convent, called Martine Dussautoy, real name

Madeleine Damerment, who was actually an undercover British Agent. Her father, Charles Damerment was involved with undercover work with British airmen who had been shot down in France and because of the danger, his daughters left France, and eventually Madeleine arrived in England and was recruited into SOE (Special Operations Executive), a Second World War organisation formed by Winston Churchill, which dropped agents into France with radios and all the usual paraphernalia of spying. Another famous member of this organisation was Odette Churchill with whom Madeleine was imprisoned, after being betrayed to the Germans. Odette survived the war, but Madeleine was executed in Dachau concentration camp.

There seems to be some doubt about whether Madeleine was really at the Convent, but there are some pointers to the fact. For instance, she appointed the Mother Superior at the Convent in Verulam Road as executor in her will. After Madeleine was captured by the Germans in 1944, Vera Atkins who had recruited her into the SOE, "sent two watches belonging to Madeleine to the Mother Superior, Sister Magdalena. In the letter she refers to her as Miss Dussautoy. Sister Magdalena acknowledged their safe arrival saying she would keep them safe until Miss Dussautoy returned". The War Office wrote to the Mother Superior in 1946 to inform her of Madeleine's execution. "As Mother Superior of The Sacred Heart Convent in Verulam Road received the Croix de Guerre from de Gaulle for her work with the Free French, it may be she knew the truth about Madeleine". Madeleine's name also appears on a plaque on the wall at St Paul's Church, Knightsbridge in London, commemorating fifty-two women from this organisation who had given their lives. Madeleine is described on the plaque as having taught in a convent in Hitchin.

Daphne Mardell received her entire schooling at the Sacred heart Convent between 1937 and 1946.

"The nuns were very strict but could also be very kind hearted. If any girl had misbehaved we would have to stand outside the Reverend Mother's Office on what was called 'The Penance Walk' for a while until told to go back to class, sometimes having been "told off" by Reverend Mother. There was a mulberry tree in the grounds – not sure about silk worms though, and a few walnut trees also stood around the edge of the playing fields, and when the nuts were ready Sister Armand would sell them.

The Convent was a girls' boarding school although little boys were taken in during the first two years, through Kindergarten Class. During the war years many French Resistance Officers were billeted at the school, and although times were hard at that time, the nuns managed to feed and support all, including spies at one stage.

Sister Armand looked after Jenny the donkey, and on the Feast of Corpus Christie, following a service at the Catholic Church in Nightingale Road, Jenny would lead the procession of girls round the school playing field (wearing her straw boater adorned with flowers) whilst some of the girls would be wearing white dresses and scattering flower petals from little straw baskets.

There were two vegetable gardens tended by the nuns with help from a few of the boarders at weekends."

The Convent was demolished in the late 1970s (Daphne attended a reunion in 1977 before the demolition) in spite of various efforts to save it, to make way for residential homes, but at least part of its history remains in the name Convent Close, built in 1979.

Number 35, "Green Shutters"

Another house worth a mention on part of this site is No 35 known as "Green Shutters". The Reverend George Gainsford had bought four of the eighteen plots sold by Lucy Bennell in 1893 and this house was built on one of them. Jasper Gainsford, George's grandson and his wife, Hazel, lived here after moving out of Birchfield on the opposite side of the road. Present-day members of the family say that the original glass used in the windows was a special kind that allowed sunlight to penetrate, enabling occupants to acquire a suntan without going outside! The house is still there, but minus the shutters.

George Gainsford's extensive properties also included a number of houses on the opposite side of the road, housing some of his considerable family, not to mention curates. All of the following four houses connected at the back by gates into a piece of land giving access to St Saviour's School and the Cloisters, both in Radcliffe Road. This access has disappeared since the land has been developed between Verulam and Radcliffe Roads.

Number 17," St Aidan's" on the corner of St Anne's Road, was probably a curate's house to start with; it is a more modest house than the next three houses on that side of the road, although it still had three storeys and a cellar. 'Else', widow of the Reverend George Bernard Gainsford, died in 1938 and bequeathed St Aidan's to the Diocesan Parsonages' Board and from then until 1976, it was the Vicarage for Holy Saviour Church. The Parsonages' Board sold St Aidan's in that

Photograph of St Aidans', 17 Verulam Road taken in the 1970s/80s when it w as the Vicarage of Holy Saviour Church. "The Vicarage" is clearly visible on the gate. (Terry Knight)

year because it fell into the category of being too old and expensive to maintain. Most vicars nowadays don't need eight bedrooms anyway! Approximately two thirds of the land was retained on which the present vicarage is built with the address being St Anne's Road. St Aidan's is now a private house.

Number 18 , Verulam Road, "Birchfield", Hitchin, Hertfordshire — *a memoir by Wendy and Bill Bowker.*

The house known as "Birchfield" owes its existence to the Gainsford family and the establishment of Holy Saviour Church in Radcliffe Road in 1865. It stands in a slightly elevated position on land originally used for arable and market garden crops, to feed the population of the town before the coming of the London markets.

This was one of several possible sites acquired by Reverend George Gainsford for his new church. It was part of Mr William Wilshere's bean field in what is now Verulam Road , formerly Nightingale Lane, Green Lane or Love Lane. The site was in a prominent position on a slight rise (described by him as "a pretty little eminence") where "Birchfield" now stands. The decision to build the new church on the site in Radcliffe Road was possibly because the slope of the alternative site would have necessitated extensive ground work.

The Rev Gainsford had great ambitions for his new Ministry, requiring the purchase of extensive land and buildings both in Nightingale Lane and Radcliffe Road, but curiously "Birchfield" was not built on the vacant church site until 1883. Perhaps publication of this volume will bring more information on this period and might reveal the reason why "Birchfield" appears to be the only Gainsford property (apart from "Woodside") not given a name of religious significance alongside "St Katherine's", "St Margaret's", "St Bridget's" and "St Aidan's" (once the "Old Vicarage").

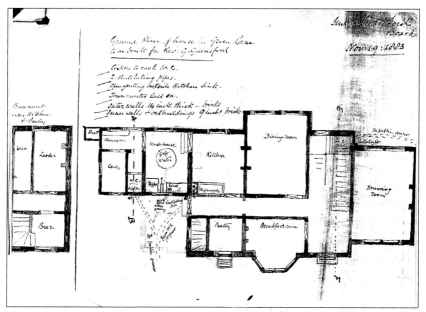

The 1883 Ground Plan for "Birchfield" in Verulam Road (Bill and Wendy Bowker)

"Birchfield" was a large family house built by James Knight a local builder and churchwarden of Holy Saviour Church in Radcliffe Road. A sketched ground plan of the house was sent to the Secretary of the Local Board on November 19th 1883, showing a kitchen, wash-house, pantry, breakfast room, dining room and drawing room on the ground floor with five bedrooms above. A cellar adjacent to the kitchen was divided into three for a larder and separate storage for wines and beer so a degree of abstinence was not expected.

The first occupier was, unusually, not a member of the Gainsford family but a retired accountant and keen cyclist, Mr Walter Morris who, presumably with his family, remained in residence until the 1890's when the house was occupied by a certain Beauchamp Victor Santry Domville, a former Captain in the Royal Munster Fusiliers. While having certain design features in common, such as ridge tiles, chimneys, sash windows and garden walls, Birchfield stands apart from the neighbouring Gainsford properties and was possibly built more in the style of the now-demolished Woodside Parsonage in Walsworth Road.

The Rev George Gainsford's son, George Bernard, also a clergyman, moved into "Birchfield" in 1898 with his wife "Else" and remained there until 1910 when they moved into "Woodside" following his father's death. During their time at Birchfield they made significant alterations to the house, extending the main bedroom (leaving a 2" step across the floor due to a miscalculation over levels). They added an entire room at the South end, now described as the Studio, within inches of the boundary wall. This room was possibly originally intended as a parish meeting room but was also used latterly as accommodation for his early motor cars, some of the first to be seen in the town. The maintenance pit used for ministering to these machines still lies beneath the studio carpet. The original plan of this room shows no garage doors or pit but an array of plain glass windows facing the road, suggesting that Mrs Gainsford may have had ideas for a greenhouse rather than a garage. The only other clue to the many and varied uses to which the studio was (and still is) put, is a note to the effect that a meeting of the Hitchin Light Amateur Opera Company (later known as the Thespians) was held at "Birchfield" on 21st February 1903.

After 1910, "Birchfield" appears to have entered a slow decline. It remained in the ownership of the family but was not occupied again by a Gainsford until George Bernard's son George Jasper moved into it from "Woodside" in 1929 on his marriage.

His wife, Hazel, raised a family of four sons here, Simon, David, Timothy and Nicholas and stayed until 1953 when they moved across the road to "Green Shutters", now number 35 Verulam Road.

"Birchfield" was divided into two in 1952/3 Numbers 18 and 18a, the original family and reception rooms in one half and

"Birchfield" today.
A drawing by David McKeeman, 2008

the domestic rooms in the other. Time has shown this to have been a successful move, making the property a manageable size and allowing some tender loving care to be expended on what is a good example of a late Victorian town house and garden. Its immediate history after the division is unknown. It stood empty for some years, the haunt of vagrants, and when a new owner bought it from North Herts District Council, it had been allowed to fall into a poor state, run down and damp. Then Anthony Ridout and his wife Janet bought No. 18 and began to restore the fabric. They regarded it as a very special place but sadly Janet died in the early 1980s and Anthony and his two boys moved on in 1986 to start a new life. We love the house and will be very sorry when Janet's skillfully made lampshades finally wear out. They are a sort of memorial to the brave Ridouts who were prepared to tackle a difficult property and recognised its many charms.

We feel extremely fortunate to be here.

With grateful acknowledgements to Audrey Eastham for her extensive research

Numbers 19 and 20, called "St Katharine's" and "St Margaret's", were most likely built for those of George Gainsfords' daughters who might need them. Not all of them married and as we shall see, even those who did, often lived in houses provided by their father or brother, George Bernard. George Gainsford bought the land on which these houses stand in 1878 and they were probably built in the early 1880s. They were built to a usual Victorian design with the 'best' rooms at the front and the functional ones at the back, including laundries which had their own chimney for the fire for the copper, and a pump for water from the wells in the garden. The houses had a bell pull system to call staff. There were indoor toilets, probably water closets, but no bathrooms which came later in the Edwardian period. "St Katharine's" had a two-storey extension for a scullery and bathroom added at the rear of the house, whereas "St Margaret's" later extension in 1909 was a more substantial three-storey one to the side of the house. At the bottom of each garden, a gate allowed easy access through the Cloisters to Holy Saviour Church in Radcliffe Road. When first built, "St Katharine's" had its own greenhouse with heating and there was also a chicken house.

Number 19, "St Katharine's"

This house has only ever had two resident families. It stayed in the Gainsford family until 1947 and has been in the Cranfield family ever since. Christabel Gainsford, one of George's daughters, lived here from 1909 until her death in 1933, and then its history becomes rather complicated. In 1934 the house was vested to Lt Col E. Bruce Allnutt,

One of the many surviving Victorian footscrapers in the Triangle at the doorway of "St Katharine's", Verulam Road

who was married to Christabel's niece, Joan. He gave it to Joan's cousin, Dulcie Spencer, from whom John Cranfield first rented it and then, soon afterwards, purchased it.

John Cranfield and his wife, Joan, brought up their three children Elizabeth, Peter and Michael in "St Katharine's." John set up his first dental surgery there, providing care for the local population, so the demands of family and business life were met. Elizabeth, his daughter, remembers rattling the gate at the bottom of the stairs, trying to attract the attention of patients in the waiting room. As well as running his own practice, John Cranfield was a post-war schools dentist in the Buntingford area. All three children went to the Convent School opposite.

Elizabeth, Peter and Michael are the same generation as Jasper Gainsford's sons and Elizabeth remembers talking to them over the wall at "Birchfield".

Michael Cranfield, his wife, Sarah and son Timothy now live in the house. On moving in in 2003, they undertook some refurbishment, including removal of the last gas lamp fittings and renewal of the electrical wiring which, it is thought, had originally been installed in the 1940s, and extended the property.

Number 20, "St Margaret's"

This house is similar to "St Katharine's, but it has had a rather more chequered history than the one next door. "Mildred Augusta Spencer, (*née* Gainsford), lived here but she had died by 1938 and apparently Dulcie Christabel Preedy (*née* Spencer) then owned and occupied the house. Dulcie Preedy died in the early 1950s after which a nursing home took it over and by the late 1950s, the Convent had bought it to accommodate their civilian staff and some of their boarders. The house then took something of a drop in fortune, as two successive owners turned it into rented bedsits and in the process, making drastic changes, removing most of the original features, building a rear ground floor extension for a further kitchen and bathroom and opening up the cellars. A family home now became 13 bedsits, including the cellars now accessed via the garden.

Elizabeth Cranfield bought the house in 2001, thus returning

Visitors from Peterborough outside No 21 Verulam Road. The car, a Singer Junior Tourer of 1928 or 1929, was owned by Wendy Cant's great aunt, her grandfather's sister, Ethel Sell. Ethel and her husband, Charlie Sell, can be seen in the front seats of the car. Wendy thinks the photograph must be pre-war, as the railings would have been taken for the war effort. (Wendy Cant)

to live next door to her childhood home, and restored it in 2005. This was a major undertaking, having to remove all the alterations that had been required to accommodate bedsits, and restoring the rooms to their former glory with marble fireplaces, picture rails and cornices, other ornate plasterwork and woodwork. The shuttering of the staircase was removed and the banisters, identical to the original, were replaced. She still finds labels in the garden from the roses that the nuns planted. Apparently the Convent's gardens were neat and well kept and they were particularly fond of roses.

These two houses have now come full circle with the same family now owning them just as the Gainsfords did originally.

21 Verulam Road

Wendy Cant who regularly attends the Triangle History Group meetings, lived here as a child with her parents, Gordon and Edith Pearmain, her uncle Derek and her grandparents. Her grandfather, Albert Pearmain, was a signalman on the railway and bought the house between 1927 and 1929. During the Second World War, her father, Gordon, was a prisoner-of-war in the Far East and she remembers his return.

"I was four years old and standing on the steps in a Union Jack apron when my father came home from the War."

She remembers everyone being very kind to her because her father was a prisoner-of-war. Her near neighbours were the Gainsford family, Jasper, Hazel and their four sons whom she remembers playing with.

St Anne's Road

St Anne's Road may have been named after the mother of the Virgin Mary and be associated with Holy Saviour Church in Radcliffe Road. A number of

View down St Anne's Road in 1995. Garden Row appears at the end, the new Holy Saviour Vicarage is hidden out of sight on the right. The two semi-detached cottages on the far left are the earliest buildings in the road. (Peter Rollason)

houses in the adjoining Verulam Road have saints' names and St Anne's Chapel in the church is a memorial to Annette Gainsford who died in 1909. The road was built about 1886 and is a turning off Verulam Road and leads into Garden Row. Only six houses were originally built in the road, but in the 1980s, a new Holy Saviour vicarage was built in the road on part of the garden of the previous vicarage, St Aidan's. St Aidan's fronted onto Verulam Road and had served as the vicarage since the end of the 1930s.

The earliest dwellings are the two semi-detached cottages on the corner of St Anne's Road and Garden Row on the far left of the picture. A parcel of land owned by Arthur Ansell was bought by Susannah Flack Mizen of Spenser Road, Brixton and later of Herne Hill, Surrey in 1884. She sold this land in 1900 to Rosa Poulton, a widow of Welwyn for £450. The site described in the conveyance was "next to and adjoining a road called St Anne's Road leading out of a road formerly known as Green Lane but now as Verulam Road." The frontage was to St Anne's Road and was bounded on the East "by a way called Garden Row" and the plot included two semi-detached cottages occupied by Arthur John Randall and Arthur J. King. It is not clear whether the cottages were there when Susannah Mizen bought the land in 1884 or whether she had them built. In 1914, a Tom Charles Poulton of Welwyn, sold the cottages to Hedley Matthews of 13 Bancroft, Hitchin for £300.

The boundary to the West was a "party wall and hereditaments of a property of Elizabeth Baron, so the land nearest to Verulam Road, where the two pairs of semi-detached houses in the left foreground of the picture stand, must have been sold in the meantime. A.J. King was still in one cottage and the other occupied by W. Titmuss. The conveyance also gives "right of way for the purchaser, heirs and assigns, his tenants and servants and authorised by him with or without horses, carts and carriages from Verulam Road, along St Anne's Road and Garden Row as far as the premises conveyed extend." He was also responsible for a proportion of the repairs of the roads.

A. and J. Allam bought the building next door to St Anne's Hall in the early 1960s for use as a warehouse. The building had been part of the St Saviour's

An invoice of 1962 from A. and J. Allam (Terry Knight

School (Infant or Junior Department) and consisted of one large and one small room. Raymond Wilshere who worked for Allam's for 30 years, remembers there were rows of little clothes pegs, each with a number and some with a child's name still visible. There was also a row of little toilets outside. The warehouse was eventually turned into a "cash-and-carry" business. In the early 1980s, the building was sold to Rollings, a "cash-and-carry" business based in St Albans. They later sold it to S & K Stores who had also bought St Anne's Hall in 1983 when the Bancroft Players moved to their new theatre in Woodside. S & K later sold the entire plot to a developer, Wheatley Homes who demolished both buildings and built the flats that now occupy the site.

Garden Row

Garden Row first appears on the 1886 map of Hitchin and most likely takes its name from the market gardens which once existed in the area. At the very end of Garden Row was the playground which led to the back entrance of St Saviour's School. A row of terraced cottages named "Cambridge Terrace" was built around 1885 and fortunately they are still with us today.

Holy Saviour's first church hall, St Anne's, stood in Garden Row and was quite used to seeing dramas and musicals within its walls; Holy Saviour Church had its own drama group and St Saviour's School also put on their performances in the Hall. When The St Saviour's School in Radcliffe Road was converted to

Children's Christmas Party 1930s. Holding Father Christmas' hand is Reg Day (who died in May 2010) and Margaret Richmond, (who died in March 2010), is receiving her present from Father Christmas. (Photograph lent by the late Margaret Richmond)

St Saviour's School Christmas Concert 1937 in St Anne's Hall. "Little Miss Break my Toys". (Rosemary Pearce)

the Gainsford Hall, the Bancroft Players took up residence in St Anne's Hall and remained there for the next 20 years.

When a Church Hall became a Theatre

St Anne's Hall, at the junction of St Anne's Road and Garden Row, will be remembered by many amateur drama enthusiasts as the first home of the Bancroft Players Amateur Dramatic Society. The group purchased the building from St Saviour's Church in 1956 for £800 and remained there until 1983, when they moved into their permanent home – The Queen Mother Theatre at Woodside.

During their time at St Anne's members converted the hall into The Players' Theatre, complete with stage, dressing rooms, bar, lighting box and scenery workshop. In addition to their shows at the Town Hall, they staged more than 30 public productions in St Anne's – their Christmas shows for children being particularly popular. With only 80 seats in the auditorium virtually every performance was a sell-out.

The writer and broadcaster **Richard Whitmore,** who joined the Players in 1951 and later headed the highly successful project to build the Queen Mother Theatre, recalls: "A great many am-dram enthusiasts must have very happy memories of play rehearsals and social evenings in St Anne's. Despite its age the old hall had a wonderful atmosphere and served us well for over 25 years. However, it had no parking facilities and in a primarily residential area the hall's ancient corrugated iron cladding stood out like a sore thumb. With the area ripe for redevelopment it was clearly approaching the end of its life.

By the late 1970s, amateur theatre had become big business in Hitchin. Some of our Town Hall shows were making profits of more than £1,000. As the Players' president during this 'boom' period it occurred to me that the time was right for the

Richard Whitmore and John Coxall standing in front of the Players' Theatre (St Anne's Hall) in 1977 with a model of the proposed Queen Mother Theatre to be built in the Woodside car park, site of the former residence of the Gainsford Family. (Richard Whitmore)

society to set out to achieve its original objective, to establish a permanent theatre in the town. By 1983 our appeal had raised over £100,000 of which £26,000 came from the sale of St Anne's to a developer. Small wonder we remember the old hall with great affection!"

Forge Close

Forge Close was built in the 1980s(?) and is a turning off Verulam Road. Nearby in the yard of the "Woolpack" public house, re-named the "Orchard and Anvil" in recent years and now sadly closed and boarded up, was once a forge operated by blacksmiths. Aquila Joseph Peacock was blacksmith from around 1910 and William Berridge from around 1925. Many people still remember Mr Berridge from the 1930s, He was a popular figure and much visited by the children of the Triangle but sadly the forge is no longer there.

William Henry Berridge, blacksmith at the last working forge in Hitchin in the yard of the "Woolpack" public house. . (Cheryl Catlin, his granddaughter)

Chapter 7

Starlings Bridge

The bridge over the River Hiz where Nightingale Road meets Grove Road has been known as Starlings Bridge from as early as 1676 and is mentioned in the Survey of the Royal Manor of Hitchin of that year. At one time, it was just a footbridge and was one of many going along Grove Path, now Grove Road. Various early maps show footbridges criss-crossing the River Hiz in this area, leading into Taylor's Lane (now Florence Street). Over the years, most of these have disappeared and only Starlings Bridge remains today. The Gas Works was built on land on one side of the River in 1834; N & P Windows ran their business from here for a number of years and following their departure to Burymead in the 1990s, they were succeeded by Classic Windows who remained until 2005. The site was then abandoned until Stephen Howard Homes moved in to build their "Starlings Bridge" development the same year. The frontage and the original side wall of the old Gas Works were saved by the strenuous efforts of the Hitchin Society and the Hitchin Historical Society. Next to the Gas Works, the "Woolpack" public house and two cottages were built in 1840. Over the years, Starlings Bridge has been widened to take all the traffic of today.

An early view of Starlings Bridge from a postcard circa 1912. Although the street layout is unchanged (apart from the roundabout), the character of the area has altered. This was a peaceful community of small traders, serving the day-to-day needs of the local residents. A stark contrast to the busy through-traffic of today.

Almshouses at Starlings Bridge: a Latchmore photograph circa 1870.
(Lawson Thompson scrapbooks, Hitchin Museum)

Charities played an important part in the life of a community before the Welfare State came into existence and almshouses are a survival of this philanthropy.

"An account of Hitchin Charities" in 1836 records

"A James Carter, in his will dated 1660, gave for the use of the poor of the Parish of Hitchin, the accumulated rents from two tenements in Houndsditch, London". With these rents, a house and about a rood of land were purchased at Starlings Bridge in this Parish; they were occupied by two poor families nominated by the churchwardens. The tenement had recently been repaired with timber felled on the property. About sixty years later, the almshouses had been sold by the Charity Commissioners and the £200 proceeds were invested to help other charities. Sadly these cottages were demolished years ago along with others that once stood at Starlings Bridge which is now incorporated into Nightingale Road. The approximate site, occupied at present by the Hitchin Chop Suey Bar, was vacated by 1886.

John Fells, Gas House and Nursery, Starlings Bridge

John Fells was born in Hitchin in 1814 to parents Abraham and Hannah Fells and was christened in St Mary's Church, Hitchin on 10th August 1814. His brother, William was also born in Hitchin, in 1816 and again christened in St Mary's Church on 20th March 1816. Their father's occupation is known to have been nurseryman and seedsman in Back Street (now Queen Street), Hitchin.

John married Rebecca Winch in Hitchin on 11th January 1836 and by 1841, they were living at the Gas House, Starlings Bridge and had a son, William, aged four. At this time, John was described as a gardener. 1851 records show that their family had by then expanded to six children. John, a nurseryman with seventeen

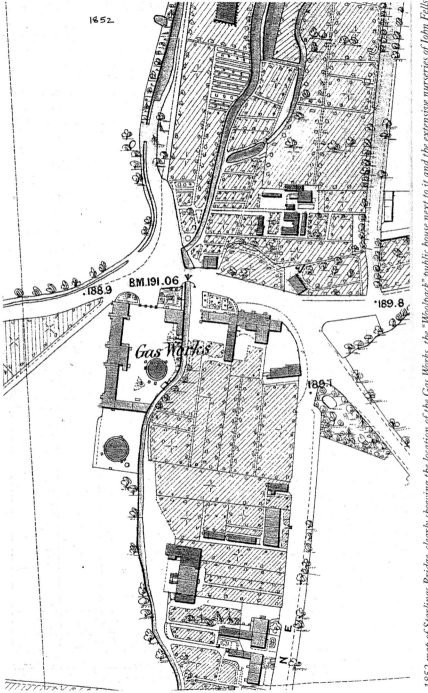

1852 map of Starlings Bridge, clearly showing the location of the Gas Works, the "Woolpack" public house next to it and the extensive nurseries of John Fells behind the Woolpack. The rectangular building opposite the 'Woolpack' and end on at an angle to the road is the James Carter almshouses.

acres of land, was employing seven men and also managing the Gas Works which employed two men.

John's brother, William, also a nurseryman and seedsman, lived with his family in Market Place, Hitchin. Twenty years later, John, Rebecca and their children were still at the Gas House, but John had become a landowner as well. Rebecca died in March 1891 and John, then aged seventy six was living with a housekeeper and one servant at 137 Nightingale Road, close to the Woolpack Public House. He subsequently married this housekeeper, Susan Ann Fairey in March 1892 and carried on with his nursery business. By 1901, they had moved to the nursery in Starlings Bridge next to the Gas House.

Brother William died in Hitchin in December 1898, aged eighty two years and his business was taken over by his son, Arthur, who was living at 23 Market Place. John survived until he was ninety three, dying on 13th November 1907.

The Fells family business had spanned several generations from the founder, Abraham in 1813. During this period, they would have seen many changes, both

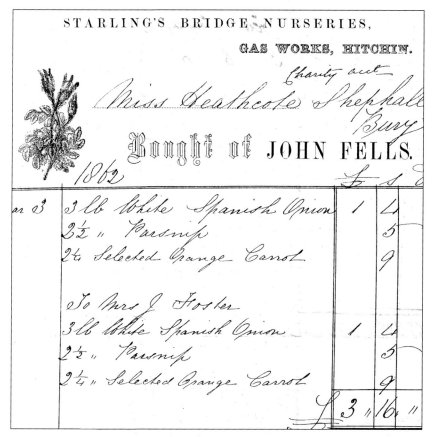

Miss Heathcote's Charity Account 1862. Were these ingredients for a nourishing stew? The Heathcote family of Shephall Bury (now part of Stevenage) were a local land-owning family

Nov 1907

DEATH OF MR. JOHN FELLS.—We regret to record the death of one of the town's oldest inhabitants in the person of Mr. John Fells, who died on Wednesday week at his house at Starling's-bridge, at the ripe age of 93 years. He formerly carried on business as nurseryman in the town, and was well-known and much respected. The funeral took place at the Cemetery on Monday. The Rev. W. J. Harris, Tilehouse-street Baptist Church, read the funeral service. The chief mourners were: —Mr. W. Fells, Mr. F. Fells (sons), Mr. H. Fells, Mr. W. Fells, Mr. Minnis and Mr. W. L. Sharp (nephews). Others present were: Mr. H. Jeeves, Mr. Noble, Mr. T. Chamberlain, Mr. W. French and Mr. James. The coffin was of polished oak with brass fittings, and bore the inscription :—"John Fells; died November 13, 1907; aged 93 years." Messrs. W. Seymour and Son were the undertakers.

*John Fells' Obituary November 1907, taken from the Hertfordshire Express (*Lawson Thompson Scrapbook, Hitchin Museum)

on their land, and in the development of the area with the coming of the railway. Local Trade Directories indicate that the family had vacated their Starlings Bridge Nursery by 1915, although a family business was still listed in the Market Place in Hitchin. John Fells' sons, William and Frederick, continued to live in family property at 149 and 149A, Nightingale Road (next to the "Woolpack ") until at least 1926. Sadly today, only the shell of the Gas House still stands and much of the land has been built on. Maps of the time show that the nursery acreage was reducing year by year as building development advanced in Whinbush Road. At least the name lives on in the small Fells Close off Whinbush Road.

Chapter 8

Nightingale Road

The origins of Nightingale Road are unknown, although it is marked, but unnamed on the 1844 map. It only existed as a muddy track or lane until it was widened and paved in 1875. It also shares some of the same information with Walsworth Road as far as field names and landowners are concerned. Nightingale Road may also have been referred to much earlier as The Walwey, being the road to Walsworth from Hitchin. Other names include Starlings Bridge and Starlings Road, a name that may have been applied to a short part of Nightingale Road in the area of the bridge. The 1844 map shows a pair of cottages with a date stone inscribed "Nightingale Cottages 1844", built on land owned by John Ransom. As these cottages were built before Florence Nightingale was the ministering angel in the Crimean War, the origin of the road name and that of Florence Street probably cannot be attributed to her and is therefore lost in the mists of time.

Whereas Walsworth Road was lined with smart villas and some large prestigious commercial premises, Nightingale Road was made up of cottages and a lot of small businesses catering to the needs of the local population, although it did have the Bacon factory, railway buildings in the goods yard and the open pasture which became Ransom's Recreation Ground.

The "retail experience" of the road is admirably portrayed in the following.

"To go to town was a treat! You didn't have to go any further than the Gas Showrooms (near where the Catholic Church stands now), you had all the shops you needed – chemists, bakers, fruit, grocery, wet fish and fried fish, Penton & Dean, the men's outfitters, butchers galore, and Herts and Beds Bacon Factory which had everything. You didn't have to go in the town unless it was Market Day!" (Gerald Billingham, born in 1929 in Midland Cottages)

Two other people recall the layout of shops in the road from the 1930s-1950s. Peter Proctor who lived from 1930-1950 with his parents at 33 Alexandra Road, drew the following plan of the shops and businesses in Nightingale Road, with the accompanying list of the owners, as he remembers them from his early years.

Plaque on the façade of Nightingale Cottages, 124 Nightingale Road.

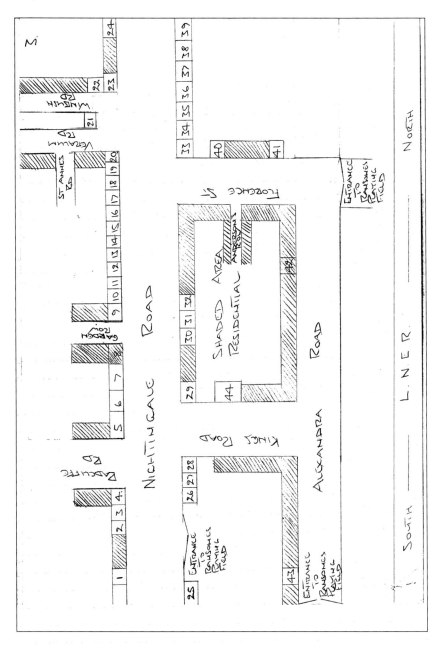

A detailed layout of the shops in Nightingale Road as remembered by the late Peter Proctor who was born and grew up in Florence Street

KEY TO LAYOUT
NIGHTINGALE ROAD AREA   HITCHIN   HERTS

1. BURROW'S TAXI SERVICE AND HARDWARE SALES
2. FURR'S FRIED FISH & CHIPS
3. HAIRDRESSER - GENTS - PREVIOUSLY LIPTONS PHOTOGRAPHERS
4. HOWARD'S - FRUITERERS
5. GLOUCESTER ARMS - PUBLIC HOUSE
6. TABNER - RADIO (SALES AND REPAIR)
7. SMOOTHY - BUTCHER
8. SCRIPS - DOLL'S HOSPITAL
9. ROACH - SHOES AND GROCERY (TWO SHOPS ADJOINING)
10. LEVITT - FORMERLY OWNED BY A MRS RIDLEY WHO WAS
                       MURDERED IN 1914
11. COX - NEWSAGENT, LENDING LIBRARY, CIGARETTES AND
                   CONFECTIONER
12. MADAM BETTINI - LADIES HAIRDRESSER
13. DOUNE & PROCTOR - BUTCHER
14. ROOD - CONFECTIONER AND ICE CREAM
15. SPICER - GREEN GROCERY
16. FENTON & DEAN - MENS TAILORS
17. GRAHAM - MENS HAIRDRESSER
18. MARSOM - BUTCHER
19. KEMPSONS - GROCERY
20. PEACOCKS - CIGARETTES AND CONFECTIONER
21. LABOUR CLUB
22. BILL BERRIDGE - BLACKSMITH
23. WOOLPACK - PUBLIC HOUSE
24. GAS SHOWROOM - SALES & SERVICE

CONT. 2.

25. BACON FACTORY
26. ABBISS — UPHOLSTERER AND UNDERTAKER.
27. ANSELL — GARAGE AND PETROL SALES
28. MOSS — GENERAL STORES
29. WHEELER — NURSERYMAN
30. CHERRY — HAULAGE, HARDWARE & PETROL SALES.
31. THOROGOOD — SHOE SALES ALSO INSURANCE AGENT
              CALLING DOOR TO DOOR.
32. COOPERATIVE SOCIETY STORE
33. CANNON — GENERAL STORES
34. DENNIS SHORT — SHOE REPAIRS
35. FURR'S — WET FISH SALES
36. NOTT — BAKER
37. WHITTAKER — CHEMIST
38. MORRISS — HABADASHERY
39. DUNKINSON — CIGARETTES, CONFECTIONER ALSO SOLD
              RELIGIOUS ARTICLES — BIBLES, ICONS ETC
              — CATHOLIC CHURCH NEARBY

FLORENCE STREET

40. THE SALVATION ARMY CHURCH
41. ANCIENT THATCHED COTTAGE

ALEXANDRA ROAD

42. BROWN'S — TAXI SERVICE
43. PEARMAN — DELIVERED PARAFFIN AND HARDWARE
              ITEMS BY PONY AND TRAP.

KINGS ROAD
44. GPO — SORTING OFFICE

Peter Proctor
22/6/95

Derek Wheeler who spent the first twenty years of his life in one of the Nightingale Cottages recalls a bustling and noisy street in the 1940s and 1950s.

56 Nightingale Road, Wheelers, florists, greengrocery, nursery and seedsman's shop

Frank Arthur Wheeler, Derek's grandfather, established this business in 1925 on the corner of King's Road on land which had previously been Massey's timber yard. (This later became John Myatt's music shop, when he moved out of the old Moss's shop on the opposite corner, although for a short while he had both shops). Frank had previously had a shop on the corner of Garden Row and Nightingale Road. He was particularly fond of growing roses and one of his sons, 'Bob' also had a nursery at the top of Benslow Lane. He still lives there, but sold off the field where the large greenhouses were in the 1980s. One of the authors of this book bought all of her fruit trees for her brand new garden from 'Bob' Wheeler in the 1970s and they are still producing good crops.

Frank Wheeler drove "a battered motor-cycle held together with florist wire" while his son, Frank Carrington Wheeler ran the shop. The business came to an end with the death of its founder in the early 1960s.

There were three other greengrocers in the road in the middle of the last century, Rainbow's opposite Berry House where the veterinary practice now operates, Gregory's near to the entrance to Garden Row and John Howard's on the corner of Radcliffe Road.

41 Nightingale Road, Berry House

This veterinary practice stands on what has been rumoured to be the site of the oldest building in the road, occupied at one time by George Cox who owned the newsagents opposite. He said there was originally an Elizabethan farmhouse there and the 1851 map shows a lot of land behind. The 1844 map of Hitchin shows a building occupying the same "footprint" as the present one, but no documented evidence has been found to verify a much earlier building, while there is a beam in the reception area with a date of 1613 it is unlikely that it is original to the building.

There were many interesting characters in Nightingale Road in the 19th Century as the following stories reveal.

An intriguing beam in the reception area of Berry House which may indicate Jacobean origin or it is more likely a later "import". (Audrey Stewart)

36 Nightingale Road, James Rennie

James Rennie plying his religious wares from his stall in Hitchin Market. James is standing right in front of his stall. (Lawson Thompson Scrapbooks, Hitchin Museum)

James Rennie came to Hertfordshire and Bedfordshire in 1872 as a representative of the Religious Tract and Book Society of Scotland at a salary of £50 per annum. He was a colporteur, the name for a peddler and seller of religious literature; Hitchin had its own Colportage Society of which James Rennie became a respected member. He made house-to-house visits in the villages of the two counties, selling his wares. He also had a bookstall in Hitchin Market for 28 years and later acquired a 'Bible van' with a gift of £50 and another donor gave him a pony to draw the van. He was also a popular local preacher and talked to village Bands of Hope about temperance.

James was born to Scottish parents in a tent in Australia in 1852 and was employed from childhood to early adulthood as respectively mill hand, farmer's lad and blacksmith. As a young man he returned with his parents to Scotland and took up his lifetime's work. His first interest in books may have been from a living-in-job as general house-boy and assistant to a general practitioner while still in Australia. While working in the smithy in Australia, he was invited to a meeting of the local YMCA (Young Men's Christian Association) at which the speaker referred to the opportunities for book-selling.

After returning to England, between 1872 and the turn of the century he had sold some 28,000 Bibles, 12,000 prayer-books, four million tracts, thousands of magazines and journals as well as other books published by the Society.

When he retired a reception was given for him in Hitchin Town Hall. He was presented with a cheque and a bible in four sections which is still in the possession of his grand-daughter, Mary and great granddaughter, Barbara.

James lived at 36, Nightingale Road with his wife Elizabeth, *née* West, his daughter and son-in-law, Helen and George Farey and their daughter, Mary. Mary grew up to be parlour maid from the age of fourteen to the Gainsford family at Woodside. She recalls that all her clothes were provided by the Gainsfords when she started; she remembers their dog called

James Rennie and family at their cottage, 36 Nightingale Road. James, with the beard, stands on the right with his son-in-law, George Farey. Helen Farey, James' daughter, is seated left with her mother, Elizabeth Rennie and between them is George and Helen's daughter, Mary, now Swain. The photograph dates from the early 1920s. (Barbara Swain)

Sixpence who had sore feet and had to wear socks when Mary took him for a walk. Later, Mary married Harry Swain and their daughter, Barbara, was also born at 36 Nightingale Road.

James died in 1926 and was given glowing tributes in the local papers as a good and respected man. Mrs Mary Swain, *née* Farey, now lives in Wratten Road, but she and her daughter, Barbara, are still interested in the Triangle's history and attend the Triangle History Group meetings.

50 Nightingale Road, Hitchin Co-operative Society Ltd and Studman & Morgan

A schedule of documents relating to this property, dated 1968, show this site was conveyed by Alfred Ransom to the Hitchin Co-operative Society in 1900 and a mortgage was taken out in 1901. The building is dated 1901 and was the home of the Co-op until the building was conveyed to Messrs D.H. Studman

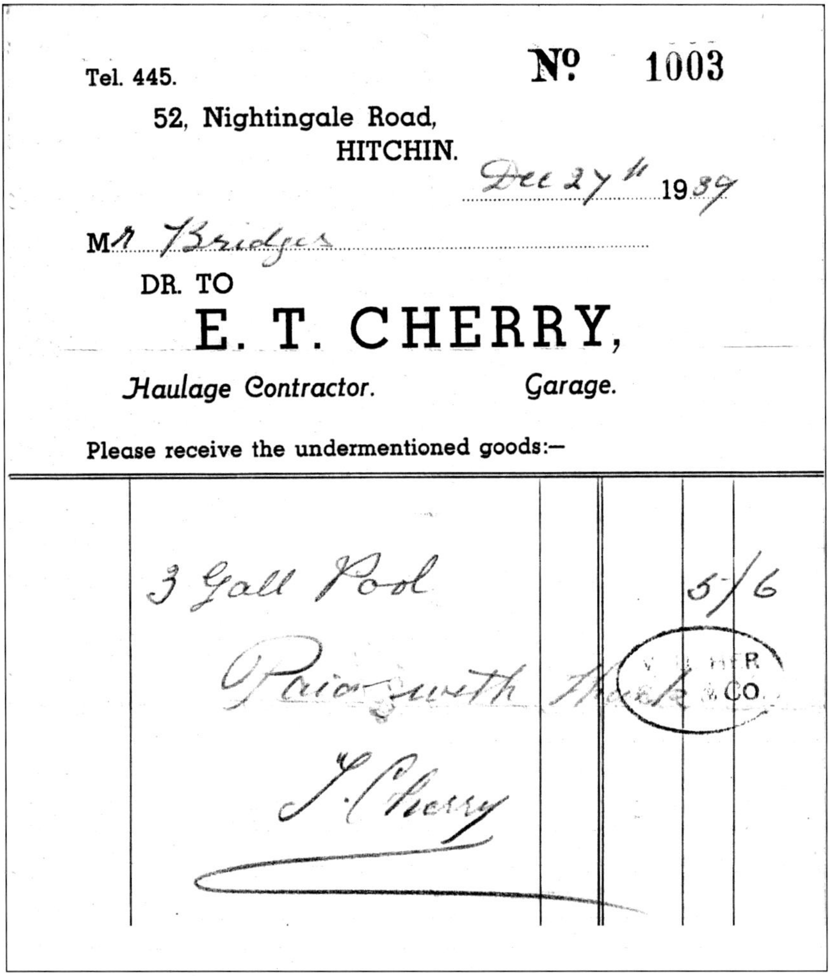

Tel. 445.   **N⁰   1003**

52, Nightingale Road,
HITCHIN.

Dec 27ᵗʰ 19*39*

M*r Bridges*

DR. TO

E. T. CHERRY,

Haulage Contractor.   *Garage.*

Please receive the undermentioned goods:—

3 *Gall Pool*   5/6

Paid with ...   ... & CO.

J. Cherry

A nostalgic reminder of the well-loved Cherry's in Nightingale Road, next door to Studman &
Morgan's. They had provided petrol for 70 years and later became a well-patronised hardware
store until 2005 when they closed for good. (Scilla Douglas)

and V.A.M. Morgan in 1968 and it became Studman & Morgan Autoelectrics.
D.H. Studman is the very same Don Studman who started his working life as
an apprentice in R.A. Morgan's in Florence Street. He recalls "Father Cherry
(of Cherry's in Nightingale Road) had a battle with me when buying the Co-
op. He ran a haulage business with his two sons (my father worked for him for
a while when I was small). Both Cherry and Ansell had petrol pumps." (Hence
the "battle", no doubt!)

Don's description of the interior of No 50 reveals the following

"There is the belief that the local LMS (London, Midland and Scottish Railway)
workers had ties with the premises and all the inside upstairs and down was painted

Recent photograph of Studman & Morgan's shop with their own van. The Co-operative Society shop was open for business here from 1901 until 1968 when Studman & Morgan took it over. Inset shows the date stone between the windows on the upper storey. (Don Studman)

in LMS colours – cream and brown. Always gave the impression of being in a railway station of those times. I also was told that they had meetings upstairs – there was a large collection of wooden chairs up there when we bought the place"

116 Nightingale Road, John Moss and son, William, Grocers and Drapers

John Moss, the founder of the large and successful grocery business, opened this shop which combined grocery and drapery on the corner of Radcliffe Road opposite to the present Molly Malone's public house in 1871. He was born in Aylesbury, Buckinghamshire in 1816 and the family moved to Cambridge where John worked with his father, a travelling draper in Cambridge, Essex and Hertfordshire. After his father's death in Cambridge, John obtained a situation in London, working very hard as a grocer's porter. He first appears in Hertfordshire in 1840 in Codicote, starting in business as a travelling draper. It was here that he met Emma Crane who lived with her family at a butcher's shop. John and Emma married in Hitchin in 1841 and the 1851 census show them living in Middle Row, Stevenage. He opened his shop there at the time the railway work was starting and a report in the Herts Express of 1903 states that "He served the navvies with hot coffee every day from Deards End to the Wymondley cutting and made a good thing out of it".

John and Emma moved to Hitchin in 1858 and John worked as a travelling draper for Mr John Smith Rose in the Market Place, premises later occupied by Mrs Campion Dawson's shop and even later, Spurrs. "Soon afterwards, he took a shop in Bancroft, previously occupied by Mr Meadley and where the police station later stood. His wife, Emma, managed this while he worked with Mr Rose". Presumably this is where the couple also lived.

For the Breakfast Table.

For the Picnic.

For the Banquet.

Moss's Home-Cured Hams

are a Delicious Delicacy.

Every Ham cut from hogs fed in this well-known Neighbourhood and slaughtered **on our own Premises.**

We are sending these Hams to all parts of the United Kingdom and the repeat orders we are constantly receiving form a most gratifying testimony to the excellence of our Hams and the universal satisfaction they give.

Every Ham Guaranteed.

W. B. MOSS,
Ham and Bacon Curer,
HITCHIN.

SLAUGHTER HOUSES, CURING FACTORY, AND STOVES, PORT MILL, HITCHIN.

Branches—

**HIGH STREET, HITCHIN.
NIGHTINGALE ROAD, HITCHIN.
AYLESBURY STREET, FENNY STRATFORD.
MARKET PLACE, OTLEY.**

An advertisement from the 1897 Hitchin Directory for W.B. Moss's shops, emphasising the ham and bacon curing side of the business.

John devoted much of his time to church work for the Methodist Church and in 1875 retired from the business altogether. He took up the Assistant Overseerships of Ippolyts, King's Walden, Offley, Great Wymondley and Lilley and even found time for tax collecting in addition. He spent his last days at 6 Bedford Street, a widower, his wife Emma having died in 1898, and he himself died in 1903, aged 87.

After small beginnings and much determination on the part of the founder, this business expanded greatly under his son, William Benjamin. William was first apprenticed to Mr Rose, but took over the grocery and drapery business in Bancroft Street in 1868, when he was only 24 years of age. By 1927 there were 12 branches in the area and a warehouse in Portmill Lane where tea was blended and packed and bacon cured. Other members of the family went into the grocery business and there were shops in various parts of the country.

Before the end of the 19th Century, William had bought the old Trooper's Inn at the head of Bancroft, the corner of the road which came to be called Moss's Corner. By the 1880s the drapery side of the business seems to have been discarded and the focus was on grocery and tea dealing.

57 Nightingale Road, William Moss, Grocer

In 1905 William Moss built another branch of the grocery at No 57 Nightingale Road, on the corner of King's Road which continued until the 1970s, when it became John Myatt's first music shop. John Myatt gave up this shop a few years

The building originally occupied by Moss's Grocery Shop at 57 Nightingale Road where John Myatt later opened his music shop. (Bill Palmer 1995)

Detail of the tiled decoration along the front of 57 Nightingale Road.

ago, a short while after moving to Wheeler's old shop on the opposite corner. No 57 is at present standing empty.

No 116 was demolished in the early 1980s around the time when some of the terraced cottages in Radcliffe and Dacre Roads were demolished and re-built.

William Moss's grocery at 57 Nightingale Road apparently had a wonderful interior with good quality furnishings and attractively arranged wares. He had a fleet of delivery bicycles and vans.

Derek Wheeler remembers that Ivy Roach's grocery, **125/126 Nightingale Road** on the opposite side, was rather more eccentric, with a "counter like a theatre set", various wares being formed into a 'proscenium arch'. Her mother had a shoe shop next door and after her death, Ivy ran both shops, hopping between them so that customers in one had to wait until she had finished in the other! After the shop had closed for the day, Ivy would deliver goods in her old car which she drove very slowly (she was one of the first lady drivers in the town). Gerald Billingham, born in Midland Cottages in 1929, has memories of an illicit purchase when he was sent on an errand to this particular grocery shop.

"…I went in there and bought this little paper packet of 5 cigarettes – Du Maurier they were, I remember because they had filter tops, and that fascinated me. I'd probably read about them or some of the lads had them. Someone said "They're a pansy kind of cigarette" – I suppose ladies used to smoke them…I could only have been 13 or 14! How could I explain what I've spent – when I took the grocery home?... I know I was in trouble…

There were four butchers, Proctor and Dolings opposite Berry House, Marsons, the Co-op. butchery department opposite the Woolpack and Mrs Smoothy's opposite Nightingale Cottages; she had a slaughterhouse in the yard where Gerald remembers that "the blood used to run out into the gutter, where it disappeared". What with this, the Bacon Factory slaughterhouse and animals being driven up and down the road it must have been a mess at times as well as noisy.

Opposite Florence Street there was Burnett's antique shop, Penton and Dean's gents' outfitters and suppliers of school uniform and scouting equipment; this shop subsequently became Worbey and Kingsley, electrical contractors. On the corner of Florence Street, there was a tobacconist's, Furr's wet fish shop, the Co-operative butchery, Nott's bakery and Whittaker, the chemist, who only made up private prescriptions and Mrs Williams' haberdashery and corsets. By the Hiz Bridge, Mrs Dunkinson's sweet shop also sold ice-cream. Opposite, between Radcliffe and Dacre Roads, was the much – loved Furr's Fish and Chip Shop. "Fishy Furr we called him", remembers Gerald Billingham, "A good fish shop that was – 1d or 2d of "scrumps", which was the batter when it comes off the fish and chips! They used to have a sieve and take off the grease…"

The cottages next door to the Woolpack housed the Red Cross Centre where electrical massage for muscular problems was performed.

There were three hairdressers, 'Madame Bettina', real name Betty Spary, Fred Rivenell near the junction with Radcliffe Road and Mr Trussell's (which still had gas lighting into the 1950s). Gerald Billingham says "He had a man's hair shop… he also had a doll's hospital, where all the children's dolls were mended – new eyes, hands, he would repair them". There were two garages, George Ansell's, formerly Issot's and Cherry's.

The imposing and rather stark entrance to Ransom's Recreation Ground, photographed in the 1930s. Note the smart lamps and the absence of trees. (Hitchin Museum)

Next to the present Molly Malone's was a cycle and radio shop owned by Taberner (probably one of the Taberner family at the Acacia Tea Rooms and Hotel in Walsworth Road), and later by John Gilbert of Baldock. One of the Sayer family, Bert, who was a plumber, had a shop opposite the lane leading to Midland Cottages.

Ransom's Recreation Ground

This area of land, bounded as it is by the railway, Nightingale Road, King's Road, Alexandra Road and Grove Road can still be imagined as grazing land. It was also referred to as Lee's Meadow and had the benefit of a pond, so that farmers could leave their cattle there to graze. Bill Palmer, born in 1918 in Radcliffe Road, remembers "The old changing rooms – that was the site of the old cow shed. The cows used to roam that field all the way down to Grove Road. They milked the cows there and the milk shop was just the other side of the river, just over the bridge". (Alderman's Dairy, Grove Farm, Grove Road)

In 1927, the land was given to Hitchin Urban District Council and the Recreation Ground was opened by Mrs Ransom on the afternoon of Whit Monday, 9th June 1930. The pond was removed at this time and changing rooms, the contemporary 'Wicksteed' green-painted swings, roundabout, see-saw and brass-bottomed slide were erected. Gerald Billingham remembers from his youth "…and in a little hut (next door to the Dressing Rooms)… was Mr Sharp – he was the Park keeper and he would sweep the whole length from Nightingale Road to Grove Road, pretty well daily if there were bits and pieces, picked up papers and rubbish – he would have his big broom." He also remembers that "we used to paddle in the river. I've still got a scar on my heel from broken glass. There used to be fish – sticklebacks – we used a net and jam jar". One of his recollections of the Second World War reveals an interesting piece of information.

"Occasionally German planes used to come over and drop long strips of foil to jam the radar, as far as we knew, there was no radar in the town! But into the Railway bank just near these houses (Grove Road by the bridge), the Hampshire Regiment built a machine-gun emplacement, that didn't last long…they moved away…sometimes we'd go along the Railway bank and pick them up (foil strips)".

Today, as the nation has become safety conscious, the area has become a partially fenced, dog-free adventure playground. In a Hertfordshire County Council development plan of 1951, the area is described as covering 12.87 acres, with two football pitches, each with a changing pavilion and a cricket pitch in addition to the children's play area. Further improvements were proposed in 1999 by the Herts Groundwork Trust. As reported in The Comet of March 25th 1999, these included re-profiling of some sections of the river bank, clearing some vegetation, planting trees and shrubs, creating a riverside path together with repairs to other paths and the bridge and making a bollarded exit from the car park to Grove Road. A design was drawn by pupils at St Andrew's JMI School with the Groundwork Trust and Hitchin Rivers Society

Today the entrance from Nightingale Road is heavily-used by people visiting the park and as a green thoroughfare for commuters. It has a community garden and allotments and space for playing football and other games.

This main entrance has recently been smartened-up with jet-washed pillars and new name plaques, the lanterns have been replaced and the gates painted.

Susan Dye and Wendy Bowker, stalwarts of the Triangle Residents' Association with Michael Ransom, grandson of the original donor, as they mark the refurbishment of the Nightingale Road entrance to the Recreation Ground. 20th November 2008. The pillar bears the official North Herts District Council sign. (Val Taplin)

The work has been done by North Hertfordshire District Council as part of a plan which could include the erection of new railings to reflect the glory of the originals which were taken down for the war effort in the Second World War.

The Triangle Community Garden

The following contribution is by **Vicky Wyer, Chair of Hitchin Community Gardens**

"The Triangle Garden was started in 2000 by a small group of local residents, keen to create an open space that could be used creatively by the community. Once the site was found, and permission granted by the Council, public design workshops were held to decide what people wanted out of the Garden and what form the layout should take. Common themes emerged such as gardening organically, encouraging wildlife and the idea of the garden as somewhere peaceful, attractive and restorative.

Since then Triangle Garden volunteers have created many of the features originally planned, such as the pond, the raised vegetable beds, the willow maze, and the central mosaic panel. Some of the features you can see at the Garden today have evolved through discussions at regular public progress

The logo of the Triangle Community Garden

meetings, like the sensory garden, the orchard and the spiral earth mound. The gradual development and cultivation of the Garden has been accompanied by a proliferation of wildlife: lizards, newts, frogs, dragonflies, bats, field mice, voles, kingfishers, wrens, robins, long-tailed tits and numerous butterflies have been spotted here.

Volunteer activity days are held once a month and focus on simple enjoyable tasks that people of all ages and abilities can take part in, and which make the garden more attractive and interesting, like sowing seeds, planting bulbs, clearing nettles and spreading bark.

Every year we hold an open day, which takes the form of a 'village fete' with cakes, drinks and plants for sale, and fun activities for all ages – like 'welly-wanging' and three-legged races! Last year a wishing glade was created where people could write a wish on a ribbon and tie it to a 'wishing web' suspended in the trees.

In 2003 we held Hitchin's first Apple Day to celebrate the creation of our own mini-orchard, and to focus attention on the importance of buying food locally and seasonally – at this time supermarkets were flooded with imported apples even in peak British season. Apple Day has continued successfully every year and is very popular with the local food producers who take part and the people of Hitchin.

In 2005 a pilot project providing gardening sessions for adults with a learning disability was started at the Triangle Garden and its newly acquired allotment. This project had many benefits: firstly the participants enjoyed being active outdoors, growing vegetables and chopping back weeds, and secondly their hard work helped to keep the Garden looking good for everyone.

A 2009/2010 programme of events in the Triangle Community Garden shows this picture of Euan Gilfillan, Thea Holcombe and Christopher and Daniel Holes proving it's never too early to get the gardening bug! (Vicky Wyer)

Over the last year this pilot has been developed into a fully-funded 'social and therapeutic horticulture' project called 'Growing Ability', run in partnership with the Growing People Programme, Letchworth. The project now runs several half-day horticulture sessions a week, managed by a trained horticulture therapist, with the aim of improving the self-esteem, confidence and skills of the learning disabled 'gardeners' participating.

In 2009, the Garden started a successful programme of craft workshops, including hedgerow basketry and dyeing with natural plant dyes, run by local experts. Further workshops include vegetable and fruit growing in small spaces, and a permaculture design course. Permaculture is a design system which looks to nature's patterns for its inspiration, and has sustainability at its core. Its principles can be applied successfully to gardening and agriculture but also to problem solving in any situation. The Garden is currently working towards becoming a Permaculture Centre, providing courses and workshops on all aspects of sustainable living.

With the planned conversion of the Ransom's Rec sports pavilion taking place in 2010, the Garden will at last have a building which can be used for workshops, wet weather activities, making hot drinks and holding community meetings.

Over the years the number of active volunteers taking part both on the ground and in the organization, has waxed and waned, and there have been temporary bleak periods where vandalism and littering have increased and help has dropped off. But new people come along and interest and activity is re-kindled, and the sense of positivity and potential that the Garden brings, starts to build again, just as sap rises in the springtime."

Leicester Cottages

These cottages lie hidden behind other houses in Nightingale Road, near to the Nightingale Public House. They were built in the 1850's and probably got their name from association with the Midland Railway which brought the line from Leicester to Hitchin through Bedford. From Hitchin, trains continued on the Great Northern tracks to King's Cross in London. The local building company of Ellis and Everard arrived in Hitchin as a result of the Midland Railway in 1857.

Joshua Wilmot, Boot and Shoemaker: 125, Nightingale Road

For almost 40 years, the Wilmots, father and son, provided Boot- and Shoe-making services in Nightingale Road. In 1861, Joshua Wilmot and his wife, Elizabeth had two children and he was employing one man and one apprentice. By 1871, six more children had arrived and ten years later, the eldest son, Edwin Joshua, had also become a boot and shoe maker, presumably working with his father. Daughters Elizabeth and Sarah were in service with the Reverend Arthur Ellis, curate of Holy Saviour Church and living in Trevor Road.

Joshua died in 1890, aged 61 and by 1891, his widow, Eliza had moved with three of her daughters to Bishops Stortford. By this time Edwin and his wife, Elizabeth, with their children had moved to 134, Nightingale Road, but by 1899 they had left Hitchin altogether for Offley where Edwin was still plying his trade as a boot and shoemaker, but combined with being the sub-postmaster until he died in 1906. This brought an end to the Wilmots boot and shoe-making business, but they were only one of the many boot- and shoe-making families living in the area from the 1850s to the 1930s. Today there are none left in the Triangle.

Herts and Beds Bacon Factory

The first British bacon factory was built in June 1912 and was situated in Nightingale Road near the Railway Station. At the beginning it was called "The Herts and Beds Farmers' Co-operative Bacon Factory". It made pork pies, bacon and other delicacies which were sold in the shop owned by the factory. Pat Gadd in her book "Fifty Years of Change in Hitchin", says "The nearby residents however were not exactly ecstatic to have such a large abattoir on their doorstep". Many local people still remember from the 1930s and

Bacon factory interior. (Hitchin Museum undated)

Station House, once home to the Institution of Electrical Engineers and the Court Offices. This building was in its turn demolished in 1992 after standing empty for a few years and the Audi garage and showroom now occupy the site.

1940s the screams of the pigs on their way to slaughter, not to mention the smell. Occasionally the pigs escaped and were seen running down Nightingale Road. Did they always escape or were they let out? Margaret Richmond who lived in the area, went to St Saviour's School and the Church, confessed that she let the pigs out once when she was a schoolgirl and then ran home to hide. Bill Palmer who lived at 27 Radcliffe Road until he was about twenty one, and now in his early 90s, describes a fire at the Bacon Factory. He remembers the pigs squealing! Gerald Billingham also has memories of the Bacon Factory.

"Herts and Beds Bacon Factory, now the Audi Garage… had a lovely big front shop, one side was all their meat from the factory and the other was groceries, biscuits, etc. As a schoolboy, I'd go in there and get two pennyworth of broken biscuits… in glass-fronted tins. It was a treat, I must admit!…at the back, they even made pork pies… but down one side, where the pigs were brought in squealing and hollering, there was a big long gantry where they were hung up, I'm afraid still alive, and they were gradually electrocuted, cut up and cleaned and all singed parts taken off. The big doors at the end were nearly always open… the smell, I suppose".

The Comet newspaper of 26th November 2009 mentions the Bacon Factory from their files of fifty years ago.

"Thieves had their noses in the trough when they broke into a bacon factory in Hitchin and made off with a safe containing £214 and even a single shilling left in the till. Before finding the till, they broke four doors, one of which was a solid fridge door. The mob was thought to have used a factory truck to haul the safe to a waiting vehicle and deadened the sound of loading it by using butchers' overalls left hanging up in the building." Ram-raiding is obviously not a new phenomenon!

The Herts and Beds Bacon factory was demolished in 1970 and an office block known as Station House built in its place in 1980. The new building was occupied by the Institution of Electrical Engineers with the County Court on the top floor until 1984 when they moved to Old Park Road. The IEEE then expanded into the top floor as well and remained there until the lease ran out. Station House has now gone and the site is occupied by the the Hitchin Audi Showrooms Centre and MacDonalds.

Midland Cottages

Midland Cottages were constructed in the 1850s as railway workers' houses on an unmade road adjacent to the former Midland Railway goods yard and engine shed. The cottages can be reached either through the Ransom's Recreation Ground or by the small lane off Nightingale Road, next to what is now MacDonald's. Until comparatively recently, they were occupied by Railway employees and their dependents, and strong bonds of friendship and mutual support were forged. Work was sometimes hazardous and tragedy could strike. Gerald Billingham, born at No 10 in 1929, lived there until 1969. His father was a train-driver who later became a boiler-smith, working on the engines.

"He'd be called out in the middle of the night for an accident on the Railway, they used to take out the brake train that was always in the siding, and they'd go round and throw stones at your windows – "Sam, you're wanted" any time of the day or night. Had to get up and go, and come back whenever they'd finished".

"At the top of the road were some horses and stables – they were the Railway horses, because they had big flat wagons that they used to pull along in the Station yard, and pick up stuff and take it into town".

In the 1940s, Pierson's coal merchants also had their stables in the lane leading to these cottages; there were few cars in the town in those days, but still a lot of horse-drawn vehicles.

Next door to Gerald at No 11 lived the Gentle family. Mr Gentle was a plate-layer "a lovely man" who used to invite his young neighbour in to listen to boxing matches on the radio (a real treat). Tragedy struck the family when in thick fog, the plate-laying 'gang' working at Cadwell, failed to hear an approaching train. Mr Gentle was killed "he was only 30 or 40 if that".

Mr Baker, the Station Master, lived at No 12A (he wouldn't call it 13) and "grew great big dahlias, he was a really good gardener"

Young Gerald and his friends had a keen interest in their immediate surroundings.

"Often I was caught trespassing on the Railway, I was a train-spotter in my youth…there were Railway police in plainish uniforms… they knew who we were. Father had warned us many times that he would lose his job if I was caught. We didn't do it naughtily, we only trespassed on the edge… we went into the little hut where the 'shunters' were…they had a lovely big fire, and we knew them all."

The cottages have survived to become attractive homes, some with modern extensions and in-fills have been made, but in a complementary style. The wooden fence in front of them marks the original boundary of the Midland Railway land.

Midland Cottages are on the register of important local buildings.

Station Yard 1997. Top left Coal Office. Top right Goods Depot. Bottom LNER Goods Yard.
(Bill Palmer)

The Railway Goods Yard

The Goods Yard in Nightingale Road still survives on the west side of the main line. The Midland Railway Company had a water tower at the top of the lane leading to Midland Cottages and on the other side of the lane was the railway yard with a turntable, loco sheds, coal dumps and offices occupied by various businesses of the town. The town weighbridge was also in the yard as was Franklin's corn, seed and animal food warehouse.

Gerald Billingham remembers the Polish train during the Second World War.

"There was a little single line that went to a turntable there, and in the War, there was a Polish armoured train stationed there, two of the officers were billeted down here (in Midland Cottages) and the men slept in the big carriage that went with it, a big gun-carriage and a tank engine that took it up and down. They'd go off for a couple of days…it was stationed at the turntable so that they could turn it round…that's where MacDonalds is now"

The yard still contains some interesting if dilapidated railway buildings.

The yard was also home to a Midland engine shed of 1860-1890; unfortunately this was demolished a few years ago and the site is now occupied by Macdonald's. The Goods Yard is on the register of local important buildings.

*Top: Midland Railway locomotive on the turntable in the yard in Nightingale Road. (*Stuart Sanders in the mid-1950s)
Below: Midland Railway Weighbridge 2003-2004. (Ashley Walker)

Chapter 9

Florence Street

The origins of Taylors Lane, marked but not named on the 1818 plan of the Town Parish of Hitchin, are unknown, although it's possible that the lane goes back much further, to the seventeenth century. It was known as Taylors Lane until 1889 when it was officially re-named Florence Street.

The oldest properties in the street were two thatched cottages built in the eighteenth century. In the 1880s they were occupied by Mr James Reid and Mr Joseph Symonds and described as "pleasantly situated in Taylors Lane." The

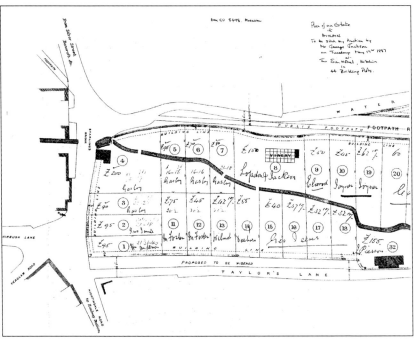

Fascinating auction plan of 1887, showing building plots for sale in Taylor's Lane (Florence Street) and Grove Mill Path (Grove Road) area. Note the footbridges over the River Hiz. The buyers' names include those of three well-known Hitchin builders, Foster, Wilmot(sic) and Jeeves. Plot 32 shows the pair of thatched cottages. The vinery in Grove Mill Lane is on the site of the recent Garden Centre, and at the time of going to print, is about to be developed. (Hitchin Museum)

cottages consisted of two bedrooms, large living room, wash house and pantry, with wood barn to each. In 1881 the cottages were put up for auction and bought by Mr Thomas Gorham Pierson for £155. The 1851 map shows the River Hiz running along the bottom of the gardens of these two cottages. In 1999 they were destroyed in a catastrophic fire sparked by a teenager's thoughtless curiosity. He was walking home with friends when they passed the low hanging thatch on the homes in Florence Street and wanted to know what would happen if he put a light to the thatch! Within minutes the fire took hold. Instead of running away, the youth pounded on the doors of the houses to get anyone out while a friend called the fire brigade. The buildings were insured for £100,000, but were totally destroyed. Most of the occupants' possessions were not insured and were also destroyed in the fire. The cottages, numbers 19 and 20 Florence Street were Grade II listed buildings. Today, town houses occupy the site where the cottages once stood.

Anderson's Row, a row of "two up, two down" cottages was built at right angles to the street in a pattern of four, then a passage-way, then another six cottages. They shared two pumps for water.

William Anderson was a builder, carpenter and joiner, with premises variously in Trevor Road, Station Road and Bucklersbury. As well as Anderson's Row in

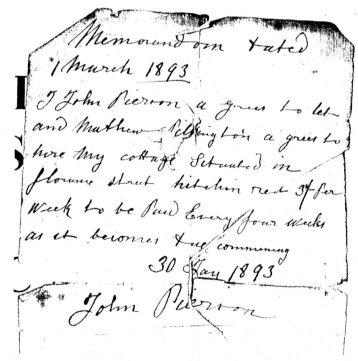

Rental agreement of 1893 associated with one of the cottages. It reads: "I John Pierson agree to let and Mathew Pilkington agrees to hire my cottage situated in Florence Street Hitchin rent 3/- per week to be Paid Every four weeks as it becomes due commencing 30 Jan 1893" (Mrs Wheeler)

Thatched cottages in Florence Street, probably 18th Century, thoughtlessly destroyed by fire in 1999. (Bill Palmer, 1995)

Florence Street, he also owned properties in Walsworth Road and Nightingale Road. William died in 1914 and all his properties were put up for auction by auctioneer, John Shilcock. There was a large attendance of intending purchasers and investors. Some of his properties were bought by members of his family, others were bought by local builders, George Butterfield and James Knight, including properties in Nightingale Road and Walsworth Road. Even with the withdrawal of some properties in Florence Street, William's estate amounted to £5,960, a tidy sum in those days.

Greta Underwood, (*née* Upchurch), was born at 11 Anderson's Row in February 1921 and lived there until she was fourteen when the family moved to Ickleford Road. She remembers there being sixteen cottages and the first four were occupied by workers at Wallace's Dairy in Bancroft next to where Regal Chambers now stands. These four cottages were owned by Mr Wallace, a farmer and owner of the dairy. She remembers the passageway which led into the back gardens looking over to the back of the Post Office Sorting Office in King's Road. The cottages had no electricity and only gas for lighting. The lamplighter used to come in the evenings to light the street lights. Across the yard at the back, there was an outhouse for each cottage, which the residents called the 'barns'. Each one housed the toilet, storage for coal and a copper for washing clothes. When Greta was very young, water had to be carried from the pumps to fill the coppers on wash-day, but later a tap was installed in each 'barn' which must have made life a bit easier for the women doing the washing.

In 1985, the cottages were demolished by the Council to make way for a residential home for the elderly, which bears the name "Anderson House". A brass plaque inside the dining area of this attractive development, reads

"The Extra Care Sheltered Housing Scheme for elderly persons was commissioned and designed by North Hertfordshire District Council and formally opened on 3rd October 1985 by Sir George Young BT, MP, Parliamentary Under-Secretary of State for the Department of the Environment.

Michael Tatham

Chairman of the Council"

The Salvation Army

The Salvation Army had been founded in London in 1865 when a Minister, William Booth, decided to take his message to the streets. He realized that the very poor often felt uncomfortable in the churches and chapels of Victorian England. In 1884 some Salvation Army officers arrived in Hitchin, setting up a 'training caravan' on Benslow Hills. They were soon invited to Ickleford where the important Ryder family offered them a barn for their services. From the start, local people were divided about their presence, but no-one could deny that Hitchin had problems. The Salvationists held their meetings in the Market Place on Saturday evenings and their 30 strong contingent was supported by their leader, Captain Taylor, on a cornet. Rowdy crowds pelted them with eggs and worse and traders grumbled about the noise. In October 1887, the Salvation Army announced plans to erect a purpose-built headquarters on former nursery land in the Taylors Lane area of the town, now Florence Street. It was to cost £700 including the plot and would seat 500. By April 1888, the new barracks was complete. Extra police were drafted into the town in case of trouble at the opening ceremony, but happily times were changing.

Foundation stones laid in the wall of the Salvation Army Hall in Florence Street. Commandant H.H. Booth was the son of the founder of the Salvation Army, William Booth, J P Drewett was the Quaker headmaster of the private Woodlands School in Bancroft, and an "Army" sympathiser.

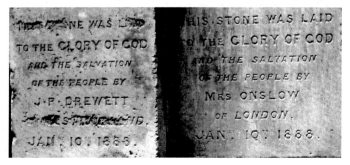

The former Salvation Army Barracks during its time as a storage depot for Waters' Removals. (Bill Palmer).

On the following Sunday, huge congregations filled the new building and 500 sat down to a "public tea". Now firmly established in their Florence Street barracks, they worked tirelessly in the community until the end of the 1960s when they left the town.

The building became a store for a local removals' firm, Waters & Sons, and was later transformed into housing and called Lantern Court.

R.A.Morgan(Electrical) Ltd

Don Studman who provided the details for this account started as an apprentice at Morgan's at the age of fourteen at the outbreak of the Second World War. He was paid two shillings and sixpence a week, in today's currency twelve and a half pence.

Reginald A. Morgan came to Hitchin in the early 1930's with £30 in his pocket and a box of tools and started repairing magnetos in a garden shed. These are devices which power the spark plug in petrol engines. He moved to a shop in Nightingale Road, but there was little space to work on motor vehicles, so when a large wooden building blew down in Florence Street, he purchased the plot from J. Deamer and Sons, the garage and removals firm. A purpose-built garage was constructed for him on the plot by Charles and Ralph French of Whinbush Road. This consisted of two large bays with metal roll-up shutters, a shop and workshop.

Don tells of the following interesting detail. "While the work was going on a decision was made to record the names of all involved in the building on a piece of paper which was placed in a match box and sunk in the brickwork; sadly, the location was not recorded."

Don paints a vivid picture of the life of the business at that time. Apparently Mrs Morgan collected the glass accumulators from many owners of battery radios "pulling a rather noisy flat four wheeled trolley with cast iron wheels" Another of his memories is how he went every mid-morning to collect Moss's pork pies and a jug of coffee from Mr Cannon's grocery shop on the corner of Florence Street and Nightingale Road. There was little heating in the garage and hands and tools had to be regularly warmed upstairs; snow used to come through the corrugated roof and had to be swept from the floor.

Car batteries were stored at Morgan's and charged every month while the car owners were away, presumably at the war.

Mr Morgan was also a volunteer fireman and during the blitz spent time in London fighting the fires. He was obviously a versatile man and saw opportunities for new business and different types of work. He took on work repairing motor cycle magnetos for the army and installed a lathe for light engineering work. Don relates the following humorous occurrence one day while working on this lathe.

"...I saw a German Dornier bomber come out of the clouds heading for Letchworth. I knew there were two men with a twin Lewis gun posted on the roof of the Irving Air Chute factory in Icknield Way. I imagined them blasting away at the bomber, but not so – later we heard that the gun had a canvas cover laced over it to protect it from rain and by the time this had been removed, the bomber must have been back over the North Sea."

The lathe work overtook the vehicle work and soon new lathes were installed. The business grew with a contract for making parts for the Admiralty and tools for munitions factories. Extra staff were drafted in by the Ministry of Labour from the Ascot Training Centre in Letchworth. (This had started as a factory making Ascot cars and motor cycles and became the Training Centre and later the Skills Centre). These included a grocer, a debt collector and a chicken farmer from Bishops Stortford who cycled home at weekends to help his wife with the chickens. Morgans also secured a contract for making metal parts for De Havilland's Mosquitos. The demand was so urgent that the staff often worked through the night making it necessary to form a permanent night shift; this work kept the firm busy until the end of the war.

Things changed however when Reg Morgan left and Albany Engineering took over and brought in a new foreman. This company had been bombed out of Croydon and when the war was over, they planned to return there. Don refused an offer to go with them, Reg Morgan returned and the premises were back in business as Auto Electricians. Changes were made to the building with a store above the garage necessitating the raising of the roof. "Also the large square clock that was on the front had gone; it had been supplied by the Dagenite Battery Company as an advertisement, but the clock was not without its problems. After a power cut, someone would have to go out with a ladder to reset the hands. It had two faces to be seen, one from each approach, but both sets of hands would never read the same; one side would read fast and the other slow, so we always had the preference as to the side we arrived by and the one for going home"

Mr Morgan acquired Mr Cannon's grocery shop on the corner of Florence Street and Nightingale Road to be let as an accessory shop, and the Salvation Army Hall next door.

New skills had to be acquired with changes in motor vehicles, such as the fitting and wiring of heaters, radios, screen demisters, indicators and fog and spot lamps. By the nineteen sixties, however, the accessories were fitted in the factories and work at Morgans had slowed. Only two staff were left in the workshop and they decided to start their own business elsewhere. Don ponders today…"Now standing before that shabby deserted building (the shutters replaced with two rotting pairs of wooden doors with peeling paint), it would be very difficult for anyone to know of its history and to imagine the incessant noise; the hum of the lathes, the monotonous rumble of the mechanical hacksaw machine and over all that Music While You Work blaring out from the speaker ….of the old Cossor radio, all of which continued on in that building day and night during those years…."

Since Don wrote this piece the building has been demolished and replaced by a block of flats to be called Morgan Court.

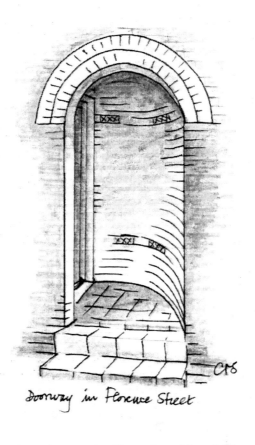

Doorway in Florence Street

*A curved outer porch in Florence Street. Master builder
George Jeeves built a number of semi-detached cottages
with these distinctive porches. Was the shape to exclude
draughts or merely one of his favoured designs?*

Chapter 10

King's Road

In the 19th century, John Ransom owned a parcel of land known as Pope's Field and it was occupied by someone called Gascoigne. The building of the road did not start until the early part of the 20th century; it was originally known as Pope's Close. The other names suggested were King Edward Street, New Century Street and Dove Street. It was changed to King's Road only a few months later.

Attractive lintel in King's Road

Curious date stone on a house in King's Road. Is it a mason's mark or builder's or owner's initials?

The Post Office Sorting Office disfigured by scaffolding prior to being demolished in the late 1990s

Different builders were responsible for groups of cottages in this road as in Alexandra Road and Florence Street. Each of them left their mark in some style or decorative feature.

The busiest part of King's Road in the middle of the 20th Century must have been the Post office Sorting Office which later became the depot for the Post Office and telephone engineers' vans and a store.

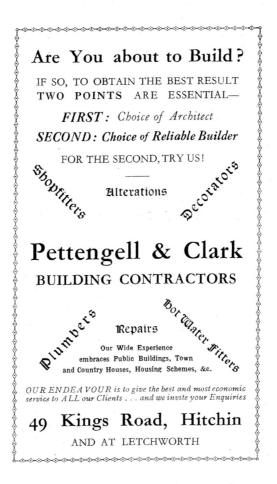

Advertisement from the Hitchin Official Guide of 1921. One of the numerous builders based in the Triangle at this time.

Chapter 11

Alexandra Road

The 1844 map shows that Alexandra Road originally spread across two fields named Pope's Field and Sword Close. The landowners were Joseph Ransom and William Curling. Today, the road runs across the bottom of King's Road and Florence Street. The road was probably named after Queen Alexandra, consort of King Edward VII who was crowned in 1902. She was Princess Alexandra of Denmark before her marriage to the then Prince of Wales in 1863. The road was planned at the beginning of the Edwardian era, but not named until 1908. An alternative proposal was that it should be named Gordon Road after General Charles Gordon, but this was eventually rejected.

Careful observation can still reward the searcher for interesting 'street furniture' such as this stop valve for water in Alexandra Road.

(Below) Cottages were often built in groups probably constructed by different builders.

Chapter 12

"Time, Gentlemen, Please ! "

The townsfolk of Hitchin have had a long and enthusiastic relationship with beer and its consumption and why not, when a safe supply of drinking water could not be guaranteed until 1850? Public houses have always been a feature of our street scene, so it is no surprise to find that the explosion of development which took place in the Triangle area between 1850 and 1870, included no less than seven of them! Throughout its history, Hitchin has been home to maltings and breweries, and neighbouring towns and villages also had their fair share.

This chapter examines the origins of all the public houses in our area, in order of their seniority. Of the original seven, only four remain open today.

The Woolpack (later "The Orchard and Anvil")

Although the arrival of the railway had a profound impact on the development of the Triangle, the first beer-house to trade was "The Woolpack" which opened its doors in 1840. It was built by a wool-sorter, William Foss. Its location at Starlings

Early photograph showing the stalwart Mr Parker, "mine host" at "The Woolpack" (Reproduced in Hitchin Gazette January 1980) (Hertfordshire Archives and Local Studies)

Exterior of "The Woolpack", decked out with flags and bunting to celebrate the Coronation of Edward VII in 1902. Note the metal hoardings, most of which advertise newspapers. (Hitchin Museum)

Bridge meant that it was on the rural outskirts of the town, and early maps show a large yard and surrounding pasture. Foss leased the premises to a Bancroft brewer, John Bradley Geard, and early landlords were all described as "beer retailers", meaning that they were forbidden to sell wines or spirits. Landlords often had a subsidiary occupation. In the census of 1851, William French was described as a bricklayer, in 1861, George Hide took in lodgers, and the Parker family, who, father and son, ran the pub for fifty-five years, were variously described as "carter" and "carrier".

Day-to-day management of small establishments was often left in the hands of a wife, who was frequently a force to be reckoned with! In 1855, Geard sold the building to Fordham's, the Ashwell brewer.

By 1915, the pub had acquired a full licence, allowing the sale of wines and spirits. Interestingly, in 1938, the owner, Fordham, applied to the Urban District Council for a change of site. The request was refused. Was traffic becoming a problem, even then?

From the 1920s until 1955, part of the "Woolpack" yard was home to the last working forge in Hitchin. Ex-army blacksmith, William "Harry" Berridge, occupied a smithy just to the left of the yard entrance, which even today, evokes happy memories for many local people. One, Don Studman, recalls that "the forge was a wooden building, with the lay-out as expected in a blacksmith's shop, and it had the smell of a mixture of hot metal, burning coke and burnt horse hair." Local schoolchildren were always allowed to watch proceedings from a safe distance.

The yard eventually became a car park, and the ownership of the pub transferred from Fordham's to Flower's Brewery in 1954 and on to Whitbread's in 1961. During

WHY buy Bottles of Spirits when you can
buy Half-Bottles and Quarter-Bottles

AT

PERCY F. JONES

Phone : 226.   "Woolpack," Hitchin.
Also at OFF-LICENSE STORES, 42, WALSWORTH RD.

WINES AND SPIRITS

	Bottles	Half Bottles	Quarter Bottles	Nips
Whiskies				
Black & White ...				
Johnnie Walker ...				
White Horse ...	12/6 ...	6/6 ...	3/6 ...	1/4
Dewars ...				
Dunvilles & Jamesons ...				
Gins				
Booths	12/6 ...	6/6 ...	3/6 ...	1/3
Seager Evans ...	12/6 ...	6/6 ...	— ...	—
De Kuypers Hollands ...	13/6 ...	7/0 ...	— ...	—
Rum Kinlochs ...	12/6 ...	6/6 ...	3/6 ...	2/9
Brandy				
Martell's * * * ...	17/0 ...	9/0 ...	5/0 ...	—
Longenck Cognac ...	17/0 ...	9/0 ...	5/0 ...	3/0
Ports				
Sandeman's Ruby ...	5/0 ...	2/9 ...	1/6 ...	—
Sandeman's White ...	5/0 ...	— ...	— ...	—
Kinloch Legality ...	4/0 ...	— ...	— ...	—
Auswin, Port Type ...	3/0 ...	— ...	— ...	—
Drawbridge	2/6 ...	— ...	— ...	—
Sherries				
Sandeman	5/0 ...	— ...	— ...	—
Wincarnis and Hall's Wine	5/0 ...	3/3 ...	— ...	—
Piccadilly Cocktail ...	10/6 ...	5/6 ...	— ...	1/2
Grave's White Wine ...	4/6 ...	— ...	— ...	—

E. K. & H. FORDHAM, LIMITED
ASHWELL ALES AND STOUT

	Per dozen Pints		Per dozen	
Pale Ale ...	Pints 9/6	Half Pints 6/0		
L.B.A	,, 7/0	,, 4/0		
Stout	,, 8/0	,, 5/0		
Brown Ale ...	,, 7/0	,, 4/0		
Very Strong Ale ...		,, 8 0		
Bass, Guinness & Worthington	,, 11/0	,, 7/0		

*"Woolpack" landlord, Percy F. Jones also ran
an off-licence at 42 Walsworth Road
(Hitchin Directory 1931)*

William Berridge in his smithy. (Cheryl Catling, his granddaughter)

the 1990s, "The Woolpack" hit hard times.
It closed its doors briefly and re-opened
as "The Orchard and Anvil", a name
harking back to happier, more prosperous
times. Despite valiant efforts however, the
decline became terminal, and after 168
years of trading, the shutters finally went
up in 2008. As we go to press, there is no
definite news of its future.

Railway Inn (Railway Hotel, Talisman, Jeans, now Lyon Court, an office block)

"The Railway Inn" must have been a
welcome sight to travellers alighting from
their new mode of transport in Hitchin.
The Lucas brewery firm in Sun Street saw
the location of the new station, surrounded
by green fields on the outskirts of the town,
as an unrivalled trading opportunity. They
financed the building of a substantial inn
and stable yard in the early 1850s, the
address being "Station Road", and by 1853
William Peck was installed as their tenant.
The yard was busy, and an ostler was soon
in residence.

The whole area was developing
rapidly, and
because of its
position at
the entrance
to the station
forecourt, the
inn soon became
a hub of activity.
Two incidents
reported in
the local
"Hertfordshire
Express"
illustrate this.
On the evening
of 20th May,
1865, a collision
occurred on the
Bedford stretch
of the railway
line, close to

An early photograph (1850s) of the Railway Inn, now replaced by Lyon Court, Walsworth Road

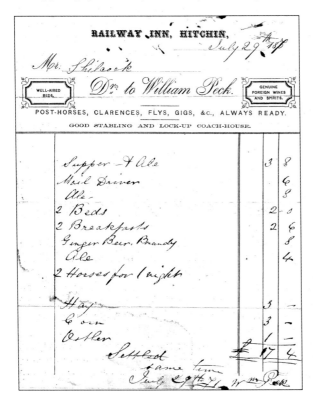

Fascinating early bill, 1871, by original landlord, William Peck. Mr Shilcock (Hitchin auctioneer) paid less than a pound for bed, breakfast, supper and beverages for two, plus stabling for 2 horses and the attention of the ostler. (Terry Knight)

The adapted façade of the Railway Hotel of the 1960s, after its transformation into "The Talisman" but before it became "Jeans" (Hitchin Museum)

Hitchin, involving a Midland train returning revellers from the annual Regatta. The injured were ferried to the inn, where they were attended to by waiting doctors, before being transferred to the infirmary in Bedford Road. Five months later, the inn made the headlines again. It was the night of Baldock Fair, and a celebratory dance was being held in a loft at the inn premises. An excess of Lucas ale caused the (literal) downfall of a participant, as he tripped on the stairs to the loft and fell over the handrail. Poor Samuel Carter, a bricklayer, sustained fatal injuries. By 1869, Mrs. Peck was landlady, and being fined by magistrates for allowing gambling to take place in the bar.

The Burton family, relatives of the Pecks, succeeded them as tenants, and expanded the business, particularly the stables. They were in an ideal position to do so. Joseph Burton is variously described as a "stable-keeper and job-master" as well as a landlord, and in 1889 could provide "cabs, broughams, wagonettes and traps ... to meet all trains". Later he added billiards to the attractions of his "Commercial and Posting House", which was now "The Railway Hotel". Burton's Path which runs from Benslow Lane to the Station forecourt and therefore behind the site of the original public house, is probably named after this family.

By the 1920s, things had moved on. The hotel was catering for the motorist and cyclist. There was a garage and "cars for hire". Bowls had been added to billiards and the main building had expanded to include the stables.

With the advent of the 1960s, the now-owners, Whitbread, sought a new image for their establishment. In 1965 it became "The Talisman", named after a famous engine which served the King's Cross to Edinburgh route. Sadly this did not halt the decline for long, because in the late 1970s, it was reborn as "Jeans", "a modern club for young people". Again, things took a turn for the worse, and complaints from residents were soon superseded by a violent incident close to the premises in 1987, in which a young man was killed. "Jeans" was closed, and

137

the building became derelict. Following a fire, it was demolished in 1991, to be replaced by the business premises known as "Lyon Court". This scheme, designed by Biggleswade architect, John Maud, for the M.J. Daniels Group of Shefford, is what we can see today.

"The Radcliffe Arms" (previously "The Nightingale")

Confusingly, the Triangle has been home to two public houses named "The Nightingale", one of which is still very much with us. But in 1855, another "Nightingale" could be found "on the road to Hitchin Station", or Railway Road as it was known in 1861. Evidence suggests that this pub became our present "Radcliffe Arms". It stood on the junction with the sometime Green Lane, which was also known as Love Lane or Nightingale Lane, the name Verulam Road not being adopted until 1883. The owners were a family named Sworder, not themselves Hitchin brewers, but with connections to both John Bradley Geard's Bancroft brewery, and a Luton brewing relative. Another tenant, Robert Sadler, is noted in 1864.

By December 1865, things had changed. There was a new landlord and a new name. William Richardson, "coachbuilder and wheelwright", wrote a letter to the "Hertfordshire Express" thanking railway officials and friends for their help in putting out a fire at his premises "The Radcliffe Arms". Interestingly, this was a case of arson, for which a serving police constable was later tried and convicted. Mr. Richardson remained until 1874, and appears to have run a lively establishment. In 1867, three "ladies" from Queen Street were arrested for a drunken brawl outside his pub, and his licence to sell spirits was temporarily suspended, and in 1869, the landlord was fined 20 shillings for "serving porter before the legal time on Sunday morning". Ownership of "The Radcliffe Arms" passed to the Luton branch of the Sworder family, and it formed part of their Brewery Sale in 1897. Tenants included a woman, Mrs. Jemima Overton, who was landlady during the 1880s. Green & Co., the Luton brewers, had a long association with the house, and peace seems to have reigned, with only minor interventions from the "Inspector of Nuisances" regarding manure pits, and ash bins.

This happy state of affairs lasted for many years.

Many have fond memories of the pub,

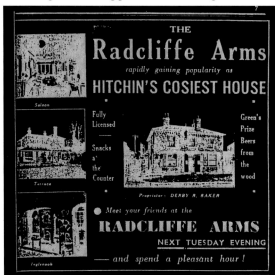

An advertisement of 1935 celebrating "Hitchin's Cosiest House", extolling its "Saloon, Terrace and Inglenook", and promising "Snacks at the Counter". "Derby T. Walker" was landlord until 1948. Green's ales succeeded to Flowers', thence to Whitbread. (Bedfordshire Express Feb 9 1935)

The site of C. John Thomson's first business venture. Did William Richardson work on this spot? (Ed Howes. 1990s)

which in the 1970s was "home" to the "Local Yokels", a lively organization dedicated to bringing fun back to the town in a way that benefited charity.

Neighbours were recently disturbed and saddened by the shabby and abandoned state of their "old friend", and fears were expressed concerning the future of the site.

During the 1980s and '90s the verandah was full of flowers and containers. Residents Ed and Nell Howes who took the photograph were keen gardeners and spent much of their time off in garden centres (Ed Howes 1990s)

Top: *"The Nightingale" in the foreground, flanked, left, by the building that was formerly "The Railway Junction Inn"* (Photographed pre 1985)
Below: *Leverett's annual outing at the rear of the Leicester Railway Inn in the 1920s. "Unfortunately we have been unable to trace Leverett's and we know nothing about them…"* (Des Aves)

Happily, in 2009, the building was bought by Sam Isaly, a complete refurbishment took place and the future of the building seems assured.

The new establishment caters not only for the "local" trade but also offers a restaurant and function room. It even serves an early breakfast! The landlord is Stuart Alder, a Triangle resident himself.

The wooden building at the bottom of the "Radcliffe" yard has an interesting history, being the first business premises of what was to become Thomson's Garage (late of Queen Street). A trade directory of 1926 lists "C. John Thomson – Motor Engineer."

One feels a natural progression from William Richardson's first use of the site as "Coachbuilder and Wheelwright"?

The Nightingale (previously the Leicester Arms and Leicester Railway Inn)

The advent of the Midland railway connection to Hitchin led to the establishment of two more public houses very close to the station, both named accordingly.

By 1859, a young Arthur Ansell was tenant of "The Leicester Arms Public House", soon to be the "Leicester Railway Inn" which we know as "The Nightingale". He was also listed as a bricklayer, a trade much in demand in the area. Contemporary maps show a generous garden plot surrounding the house, together with stables and outbuildings. Fordham's of Ashwell supplied the ale, and the 1861 census showed a boarder in residence, a mason from Derby. Trade continued peacefully under a succession of landlords, to be rudely interrupted by a major fire which took place in the yard one night in August 1903, (cause unknown, according to Fire Brigade records). A coach house, stable, barn, sheds and a quantity of loose hay were completely destroyed, but "the adjoining house and barn were saved". Occasional references to the installation of new drains and to the "clean and sanitary" accommodation lead one to believe that this was a well-run establishment.

The rise of the automobile led Henry Herbert Windley, landlord between 1922 and 1948, to diversify. He advertised in a local trade directory that he was "close to the Railway Station, has large tea gardens, lunches and teas provided; parties catered for; good garage; accommodation; moderate charges; cars for hire. Telephone No. 239". A contemporary postcard shows a long single-storey tea room, set in an attractive garden shaded by trees.

By happy coincidence, a descendant of this landlord has passed photographs and memories on to the Hitchin Historical Society to which he belongs. Des Aves ("my first memory is in the cellar during an air raid…") confirmed that his grandfather, Henry Herbert Windley, was succeeded by his son, Dennis Henry Windley who ran the pub until 1960. He also forwarded this interesting photograph sent as a "thank-you" to his grandparents and staff following a works' outing.

Flowers succeeded Fordhams as brewers, and in 1962 they applied to the Urban District Council for permission to convert to "light industrial purposes", but were refused.

On New Year's Day, 1962, the little branch-line between Hitchin and Bedford closed, making the inn's name an anachronism. By the mid-1960s it had become "The Nightingale" that we know today.

The Railway Junction Inn

The arrival of the Midland Railway at the nearby station provided an opportunity for the Lucas brewery to add to its tally of "tied houses", and in 1862 they opened "The Railway Junction Inn", not many yards from their own

"Railway Inn", and close to Fordham's "Leicester Railway Inn". Obviously there was sufficient demand, as trade was brisk from the start! George Gascoigne was the first tenant, but by 1871 the Nutting family was in residence, an association which lasted until after the First World War. In the early days the pub obviously had a very lively reputation, as in 1871 landlord Jack Nutting was fined 40 shillings for "allowing disorderly conduct and drunkenness in his house". Local "bobby" P.C. Tripp had been scandalized by a scene of drunken revelry when he had called in at 10.15p.m, witnessing men and women rolling about on the floor! Things obviously calmed down after this, for apart from a few "longstanding manure" issues, no more complaints were received.

By 1903, Pierson & Co., Coal Merchants, were sub-tenants of the yard, a convenient location for them close to the railway sidings. The establishment appears to have been a very happy one, and a favourite with railwaymen. It was apparently a local joke, relayed to irate wives, that their erring spouses "had been delayed at the Junction"! In 1908, Mr. Lucas was guest of honour at "a new Room, which could easily accommodate 150 people", and this soon became a popular venue for concerts and Friday-night dances. "The Junction "moved with the times and by the1920s was offering meals, a garage and "cars for hire". It also became the headquarters of the local branch of the National Union of Railwaymen.

In 1962, after nearly a century of trading, the pub underwent a change of use, and was sold to James Bowman and Sons, whose flour mill abutted it at the rear. Martin Priestman, the architect who amongst other work, designed Hitchin Library, adapted the pub and it became a welfare building and canteen for the mill workers. Both it and the mill were demolished in 1985, and replaced by the B&Q store.

This also closed in 2007 when a new B & Q store opened on one of the retail sites in Stevenage. As yet, this prime site has not been developed.

The Railway Junction Inn and Bowman's Flour Mill during demolition, 1985. (Bill Palmer)

Molly Malone's (originally The Gloucester Arms and then O'Shea's)

"The Gloucester Arms" or "Gloster Arms" as it was originally, was certainly trading from its present location by 1871, as its landlord, Charles King, appears on the census. He was a brewer by occupation. In 1877, George Jackson, the Auctioneer, had the following entry in his Sale Catalogue, for "King, Hitchin". "By amount realized by Sale of Brewing Plant, Radcliffe Road, Hitchin : £34. 13.0." This strongly suggests that Charles King was brewing in the "Gloucester" yard, which was at the junction with Radcliffe Road. From the sum realized it was obviously a small-scale operation, and by 1881 he was in Bancroft as a "Beer dealer".

In February 1882, the pub was named in the "Hertfordshire Express" as the venue for a local inquest (not uncommon), and from then onwards we have a succession of landlords who seemed to have served the community

TELEPHONE: HITCHIN 616.

The Railway Junction Inn

NIGHTINGALE ROAD
HITCHIN

GARAGES TO LET.   FREE CAR PARK.

The Noted House for a Good Glass of J. W. Green's Luton Beer.

Large Hall for Hire for Weddings, Meetings, Dances, Dinners, etc. etc.

BED AND BREAKFAST.   PARTIES CATERED FOR.

Proprietor: **FRED R. DANIELS**

Advertisement from the Hitchin Directory of 1937

peacefully and respectably, never appearing to fall foul of the law or the Inspector of Nuisances. As a beer-house it obviously did a modest trade, as landlords were noted on the census as having other occupations. The reason for the pub name is unclear, as there do not seem to be any obvious links, either town or railway, with Gloucester, and the first landlord had been born in Pirton!

In 1878, Arthur Ansell (we met him earlier at the "Leicester Railway Inn"), was calling himself a builder, and later, Alfred Jefferies was "a beer retailer and fishmonger". He advertised "a supply of fish fresh every day", made possible in the 1880's by the speed and efficiency of the railway network. In 1897 the house was purchased by Simpson , the Baldock brewer and in 1899 we read of another

Promotional matchbox cover, dating from the tenure of landlord Eddy ? and his wife, Wendy.
(Terry Knight)

thriving business being carried out in the yard at the rear of the premises. The entrepreneurial J.J. Burton, "mine host" at the nearby "Railway Inn", was advertising his "Gloucester Arms Posting Stables", citing his personal address as "Radcliffe Road, opposite stables".

He hired-out carriages "of all descriptions on reasonable terms". This must have been a lucrative extension to the trade in his own stable yard. Presumably Mr. Jefferies was fully occupied with his fish business? "The Gloucester Arms"

J. J. BURTON,

Gloucester Arms Posting Stables,

NIGHTINGALE ROAD, HITCHIN.

OPEN and CLOSED CARRIAGES of all descriptions and BRAKES
for hire on reasonable terms.

Private Address: 38, Radcliffe Road (opposite Stables).

ORDERS PROMPTLY ATTENDED TO.

Advertisement from "Handbook to Hitchin and the Neighbourhood" (1899)

remained a beer-house until the 1930s, when it applied for a full licence. It is now a Greene King house.

During the 1990's it was also known as "O'Shea's" and today, it is popular as "Molly Malone's". Since 2009, the Triangle History Group has met here once a month to share old photographs, documents and information, much of which is incorporated in this book. It is a comfortable and welcoming hostelry where local residents still drop in for a drink and sociability.

The Albert (formerly The Early Bird)

The friendly and compact "Albert", variously described as being in both Walsworth and Dacre Roads, was certainly trading as a beer-house by the late

Exterior of "The Gloucester Arms" photographed in 1987. Derek Wheeler, born and brought up in Nightingale Road, remembers that during the tenure of landlord Ted Russell in the 1950s and 60s "all the telephone wires as they went across the road had rubber blocks on them so that his racing pigeons wouldn't injure themselves flying into them. They were kept in a pigeon-loft at the back, and there was also a small one on the side of the building". (Terry Knight)

A happy gathering of the Triangle History Group in Molly Malone's in August 2010. From left to right standing: Audrey Stewart, Jo Maddex, Pauline Humphries, Wendy Cant, Bill Harmer, Gavin Budge, Sue Budge. Seated middle: Barbara Swain, Valerie Taplin, Margaret Harmer. Seated front: Giles Maddex, Jenny Shirley, landlord Andrew Holland, Mary Swain. (Val Taplin)

1860s, under its original name "The Early Bird". The first landlord was recorded as Thomas Estwick, who was a tenant of Simpson, the Baldock brewer, but whether travellers could get an early drink on their way to the station is not known!

In 1869, the "Hertfordshire Express" reported, with a certain relish, the on-going battle between the Reverend George Gainsford's supporters who lobbied against the granting of a spirits licence to the pub and the supporters of the proposal, led by William Onslow Times, a local "worthy" and clerk to the Local Board of Health at the time. Mr. Times had "suffered an accident outside the house and would have welcomed a glass of brandy on that occasion". Reverend Gainsford's party won, but a wine licence was granted soon afterwards.

Original foot scraper at the door of The Albert

By 1874 the tenant was Joseph Saunders, formerly an employee of the Great Northern Railway and the name was changed to "The Albert" (occasionally the "Prince Albert"), after Queen Victoria's beloved consort, who had died in 1861. The Saunders family enjoyed a tenancy of over fifty years. By the 1880s the beer was being supplied by Green's of Luton. The pub was obviously a law-abiding and peaceful one, as no mention of misdemeanours appeared in the vigilant local press!

Between 1950 and 1978 the house had no fewer than fourteen licensees, a Triangle record! In 1997, following extensive renovation, it came up for sale, but the modest and attractive exterior seen in the early photographs is largely unchanged. It is now a Free House and still serving the locals. And so we come to the end of our tour. Three of the original seven "Triangle" pubs are no longer with us, victims either of circumstance, or a changing way of life. The four that remain have each developed their own particular "character", and all look back on a century and a half's presence in our midst. Their future is in our hands. "Cheers!"

A fascinating early photograph of "The Albert", dating from early in the last century. The posters to the left of the door depict cavalry and infantry soldiers. Thomas Brooker's hardware shop can be seen on the extreme left of the picture, behind the little girls running errands. (Frank Perry, present landlord of "The Albert")

An (almost) exclusively male outing setting off from "The Albert", probably during the 1930s. (Terry Knight)

Chapter 13

FIRE! FIRE!

Tucked away in the recesses of Hitchin Museum, lies a fascinating collection of the town's Fire Brigade records. They comprise seven hard-backed ledgers, detailing "call-outs" between 1867 and 1939, when the Second World War intervened.

Between 1867 and 1939 the vast majority of Brigade call-outs were" chimney-related". Coal fires were the normal method of heating both home and small business premises, houses were often small and sparks and embers an ever-present hazard. Whether it was a spark from a copper chimney blowing through an open bedroom window and lighting the bedclothes (August 1918, King's Road), or clothing left too near a stove (November 1934, Bacon Factory), the result was the same. Sometimes, as Mr. Brown found in his clothes' shop at 98, Nightingale Road in 1926, the cost of warming his clients resulted in the destruction of his stock. Mademoiselle Baridon, working as a dressmaker in an upper room in Dacre Road, also lost her workroom owing to a wayward spark. Mainly though, these many small fires were caused by "foul chimneys", as the Brigade records baldly state. Later entries record a call-out charge of £3.

During the whole period, only one fire-related fatality occurred in the Triangle area. In February 1918, poor Mrs. Mary Osmond, aged 31 years, the invalid wife of an employee at Moss's Furniture Department, fell onto an unguarded fire in King's Road. Neighbours intervened and put out the fire before the Brigade arrived, but to no avail. Another Triangle resident had a lucky escape. In May of the same year, the Brigade was called to the shop of Mrs. Ridley at 125, Nightingale Road. The lady was found unconscious on the charred remains of her sitting-room floor, close to an overturned lamp (and an empty whisky bottle). She recovered in hospital. (Sadly, this unfortunate lady was soon to meet with a violent and untimely end, probably murder, although no-one was ever convicted of the crime).

Because of the close-knit nature of Triangle life, and the distance and poor communications between the area and the Fire Brigade, early residents employed a great deal of ingenuity when called upon. In 1913, the fire at Miss Titchmarsh's shop and sub-post office was put out by residents. "Contents of one room burnt out - £50". Although they were not involved, the Brigade drew the Council's attention to "the necessity of a system whereby the Brigade may be summoned without loss of time to fires in the more distant parts of the town". In March of the same year, neighbours dealt with a fire at the Frythe Laundry, Nightingale Road, "in the occupation of Mr. Casbon". They employed the "Patent Fire Extinguishers from Mr. Blake's Picturedrome, which were used to good effect". In August

1929, prompt action was taken at Mr. Walker's house in Nightingale Road, when neighbours threw a burning bed out of the window. "Cigarette-end found", the Record states ominously.

Two incidents of youthful mischief were reported. In 1908, there was "a slight outbreak of fire at the house of Mr. Bater in Florence Street". Mrs Bater had gone out, leaving two children alone inside. Neighbours "smelt something burning and, going outside, saw smoke coming from the windows … the outbreak was in a cupboard under the stairs." Again, they "set-to" with buckets and jugs, a timely intervention, as "the house was one of a row, there being a good deal of woodwork in the construction". In October 1924, a blaze in a shed full of stores at the rear of "Messrs. T. Brooker, Station Road", now Walsworth Road, was discovered. Luckily it was contained by the "Steamer" and the Morris Guy fire engine. Cause, "children playing with fire"!

Arson was only reported twice, although there were a few suspicious incidents. In 1938, a fire in a hedge in Walsworth Road was dealt with in three minutes. Mentioned in retrospect is the incident covered in the history of the "Radcliffe Arms", when a fire broke out in "Mr. Richardson's coachworks at the back of the "Radcliffe Inn". Arson was not proven against a police recruit named Scott, but subsequent to his relocation to another division, more fires occurred and he was convicted. Again, the neighbours had been instrumental in extinguishing the fire.

There is only one mention of a malicious call-out. In April 1939, a malcontent rang from a box in Florence Street, claiming that the "Leicester Arms" public house was ablaze. "The matter was left in the hands of the Police"….

In March 1919, the Brigade received a call from the Moss family. The basements of warehouses to the rear of their Nightingale Road premises were awash with 15 inches of water, "a mysterious affair"!

During the period covered by the records, there were four major fires in the Triangle area, and a number of others which could have easily escalated, had it not been for the skill and dedication of the Hitchin Brigade. The close proximity of both business and storage premises to tightly-packed residential areas was a matter of great concern. In the early days, stocks of timber and hay were often sited next to occupied buildings.

The first large outbreak on 3rd August, 1899 in Mr. Fisher's Sweet Factory in Verulam Road has already been dealt with in a previous chapter, as is the fire at the Leicester Arms public house.

Another serious fire broke out in August 1905. The Brigade arrived after a delay of 25 minutes to find "Mr. Sutton's stables" in Nightingale Road ablaze. In an era before much public entertainment, a "good fire" acted as a magnet to the neighbourhood. The stables were constructed of "sleepers and tarred wood, and piled high with hay", so that the fire spread quickly. They were close to the houses in King's Road. By the time that "the hose reel and manual" arrived, the Brigade was confronted "by a great crowd of close upon 3,000 people which packed the street and invaded the neighbouring meadow and trampled the crops" … the sky was lit-up by the glare, and small print could easily be read in neighbouring streets". The police were called to control the onlookers "who, as not infrequent amongst the class of whom they were chiefly composed, assumed a hostile attitude and hooted the firemen", a comment which illustrates much about the era.

Things were better controlled in October 1925, when fire ripped through the Herts and Beds. Bacon Factory in Nightingale Road. This time, the crowd was "ably controlled by Supt. J.H. Prior". The cause was either "a spark from a smoke hole or a fuse in the electric lighting system". The plant was only saved from destruction by "the manner in which the outbreak was tackled by Hitchin Firemen". Employing the Morris Guy and the Shand "steamer", the blaze was confined to the west side, a profound relief, as the other end was " in close proximity to the Shell Mex Petrol Store". Despite a gaping hole in the roof, work in the factory was scarcely disrupted.

Undoubtedly, the skill and professionalism of the Brigade was instrumental in preventing a number of Triangle outbreaks from becoming disasters. As previously mentioned, the presence of industrial premises and workshops in a residential area was a hazard. Stored timber was responsible for four fires which could have had serious outcomes. Mr. Massey's timber yard in Nightingale Road, where John Myatt's shop now stands, was responsible for several "call-outs" between 1906 and 1910. In August 1922, residents in Trevor Road had reason to be grateful when a fire broke out at a carpenter's and box maker's workshop. Swift intervention saved residential properties from damage, even though a barn at the rear of the premises was completely destroyed.

Larger industrial units in the Triangle area, where fires could have wreaked major havoc, were also recipients of help. A potential disaster in Walsworth Road was averted at Messrs. Sanders and Sons, Carriage and Motor Car Works, in July 1919. "A defective electric light wire caused damage on the first floor". "Hand pump and axes. Damage £5. Property saved valued at over £30,000". This new-fangled lighting was not without risk!

Swift intervention also prevented escalations at both the Gas Works in Starlings Bridge and at Bowman's Mill in 1928. A paraffin blaze at the former premises was put out by a chemical extinguisher and the latter was saved from major damage by the timely use of the firm's own "sprinkler valve". Indeed the Records show a greater reliance on more sophisticated methods of fire-fighting as the decades moved on. Increasing technology in everyday life was being matched by advances in the Brigade's armoury of weapons.

We leave you with a final crowd-pulling scene. On 29th February, 1928, a four-ton Saurer lorry was ablaze in Station Road. "The flames made a thrilling spectacle and reached an enormous height". A large crowd gathered, and watched the driver jump to safety. Happily the petrol tank did not explode, although the lorry "was a charred wreck....Extinguished by chemicals".

Drawing of a fireman's brass helmet.
Courtesy of Denis Dolan

Epilogue

It is fitting that the last word should be given to those who live in The Triangle or have close connections with it. It is not all about days gone by; it is still a thriving and dynamic community as the following personal contributions confirm. The first is from Judi Billing who lived for a while in Walsworth Road. Interestingly, Sue Dye, another contributor, now lives in the house in Walsworth Road that Judi used to occupy.

Judi Billing, Councillor for Bearton Ward and Chairman of Hitchin Committee, wrote in September 2009:

"I was a London girl – born in 1951, and brought up in Paddington and Notting Hill. My home was a flat in what should have been a gorgeous Victorian residence just off Portobello Road, but at that time it was closer to a slum rented to my parents by the notorious racketeer landlord and creator of slums and race riots, Mr Peter Rachman.

The notion of a world that might exist anywhere north of Finchley was beyond my comprehension.

Wind on 20 years exactly and I found myself on a Green Line Bus to Hitchin. Passing places I didn't think I would like to live in very much such as Stevenage and Hatfield I remember a sense of huge relief arriving in Hitchin and walking through cobbled lanes to find the town centre. It was summer. I was expecting my first baby in November and needed somewhere to live quite quickly. A local estate agent told me that for the tiny sum we could afford we would find ourselves living in what he described as "a black area". I was surprised both by this evident and open racism but also that he might think this a problem since I expected and enjoyed living somewhere full of different peoples, races and religions and my first home was a lovely little house in Grove Road with a corridor. This was important. Firstly because it cost £4450 rather than £3750 which was the price of a house whose front door opened straight into the living room, and secondly because it meant somewhere to put a pram!

I had 3 children in that little house, but eventually needed somewhere bigger and moved in 1978 into a large Victorian 3 storey house, then divided into bedsits, on one of the Triangle's edges in Walsworth Road. Two years later I became a councillor for Bearton Ward which includes the Triangle area and have represented it with affection, joy and occasional exasperation ever since.

Writing at a time when Hitchin's old houses are incredibly sought after and mostly cherished, when people go to enormous lengths to conserve, preserve and tastefully replace, it seems strange that at that time people craved new homes with modern equipment and the old houses in the Triangle could be really difficult to sell.

So how do I remember and describe the Triangle 30 years ago? It was the first really multi cultural area of Hitchin as home to families from the Caribbean, the Punjab, East Africa, Poland, Italy and London émigrés such as myself as well as a proud and faithful indigenous population. It was a great place to bring up small children, meet other young parents, share babysitting circles and school walks (not car runs!), and for me it was a great place to be a community volunteer and do a fair amount of politics.

It was also quite a poor place. It was little understood by those who lived leafy lives across Walsworth Road in Benslow Lane, Highbury Road and The Avenue. When I first represented people in the Triangle some homes were woefully lacking in decent amenities and some elderly folk still had homes with outside toilets and no bathrooms. Many of the bathrooms that were added were on the ground floor beyond the kitchen and as I write this I can still smell the strong whiff of coal fired water heating, and remember trips to the launderette in Nightingale Road before the acquisition of a washing machine was regarded as standard. The Straw Hatter Launderette has been there and so named for at least 37 years which whilst not glamorous must be one of the oldest businesses in Hitchin!

Some houses in the Triangle were deemed beyond redemption. These were replaced as council houses through the late 70s and early 80s, and they represent a remarkable new phase in local social housing. Considering how close in time their building was to some local atrocities they fared very well. Compared to the housing estate concepts at Westmill, the dreadful structure which became known as the Churchgate Centre and the tragic removal of the building where the Wilko building now offends us daily, the new homes in Dacre and Radcliffe Roads seemed to be a first attempt to create something which met the mood of the area and respected in small part its heritage.

Since then of course the beautiful re-working of the Gainsford Hall in Radcliffe Road has developed into a lovely art form blending the old architectural concepts with the needs of modern living in the Triangle in 2009.

The Triangle is a precious and much loved place, spirit and community. It can still be helped to flourish or be hindered by insensitivity.

It is helped by a thriving and vigilant Residents Association, well established and trying hard not to be dependent on just one or two activists who can make such organisations time-limited. It is helped by having finally decided after a 20 year conversation with itself to restrict parking to residents only, which has made a huge difference to the atmosphere of its tiny streets during the day.

But it can also continue to be hindered, by ridiculous, insensitive and inappropriate development squeezing badly designed density onto every square metre of its existence. And it can also be hindered by the anti-social behaviour of people who don't care as much as most of us about its sense of place.

For those who use the Triangle as a base from which to commute to London it can also be difficult to join in with community life, but usually they come to love it too and to contribute fully to its social and economic well-being as the years go on, and the 6.42 fast train to London becomes less attractive".

Judi's description of the multicultural make-up of the Triangle couldn't be better illustrated than by **Clarence Griffiths**. He came to England from Barbados in 1960. He arrived in London but found the big city too busy and unfriendly. After visiting a friend in Hitchin, he found a home here and has been part of the community ever since. He lived first at 46A Walsworth Road for 4 or 5 years and then moved to John Barker Place. He first worked at Kayser Bondor and played cricket for the firm, but was spotted by Hitchin Cricket Club and subsequently played for them. He then joined what is now British Telecommunications.

Holy Saviour Church Centenary Day, Tuesday 25th May 1965. Churchwardens Bill Dove, front left and Clarence Griffiths,front right, escorting the Bishop of Rochester, the Rt. Reverend David Say from the Cloisters into the Church. The Bishop is preceded by Father Thomas from St Katharine's, Ickleford, acting as Bishop's chaplain for the occasion. At the time of the Church's consecration in 1865, Hitchin was in the Diocese of Rochester, so inviting this Bishop to preach at the Centenary was a nice nostalgic touch. (Holy Saviour District Church Council)

"I was the first black man in the Post Office and also when I joined BT and stayed with them until retirement. The first thing I looked for was a church and it was St Saviour's Church". Clarence was churchwarden for a number of years, including the time of the Church's Centenary in 1965. His son, Stuart, used to serve at the altar.

"I also went to Hitchin College, doing maths, English, physics and when I joined BT, I had to stop that because I was training there with Jim Webb and Geoffrey Kirby" (long-standing members of the Church choir. Jim died a few years ago but Geoff has completed well over 50 years).

"Hitchin reminds me literally of a part of Barbados and the only differences are the weather and no sea! Hitchin is so beautiful; I had the choice of living in Letchworth, Luton, Stevenage, but Hitchin has so much history and I love that"

He has pictures of Hitchin in his house in Barbados.

Since retirement, Clarence lives mostly in Barbados, but comes back to Hitchin at least once a year. He is much loved at the Church whose choir visited him in Barbados in 2003 & the choir from St Catherine's, his church there, returned the visit when they came here in 2005. Every year when he visits Hitchin, he packs a barrel of groceries which is shipped back to Barbados for the poor, the elderly and "shut-ins" (the house-bound) for them to store in case of hurricane. St Catherine's acts as a refuge in the event of a hurricane. The Holy Saviour congregation have aso helped with this in 2010.

Wendy Bowker, who has been active in Hitchin Forum for 15 years, is also a literary person, writing poetry and regularly hosting writers' days; she likes taking her children and grandchildren to The Globe Theatre in London for Shakespeare performances. Wendy lives with her husband, Bill, at Birchfield, one of the Gainsford houses in Verulam Road; she also paints a full and interesting picture of life in The Triangle today in this piece from 2009.

The Triangle Now

Well I live on the edge (of the Triangle) and Verulam Road is often not quite sure whether it belongs to the area or not. This road is certainly regaining some of its former elegance, having gone through a period when one Gainsford property had become a seedy rooming house and several others needed a bit of care and attention. Such a pity it was ever straightened out to allow too many cars to whizz about and clatter and crash with empty containers and skip lorries. I've lived here for twenty odd years which is the longest time I have ever lived in a town being a country woman at heart. Perhaps that is a clue to life here as it is now.

Of course this area would have been a complete village with its own butchers, bakers and probably church candle makers when this history started and some of that has been lost but it still has enough shops, businesses and pubs to make it an area less dependent on the town centre and supermarkets than the smarter side of town. Maybe this is partly due to the wide variety of its residents: its ethnic mix is obvious but there is also a huge range of people from every sort of background who mix and mingle in various ways: church congregation, Triangle Residents Association, guides, brownies, various other groups who use the church hall in Radcliffe Road and if you shop at the S & K on the corner of Radcliffe Road and Walsworth Road a few times a week you will eventually run into just about everyone. That place - with its hugely varied stock and long opening hours - is a very important establishment which should be duly cherished. The area would be much poorer without it. Likewise the good old Kushma Cottage

S & K Superstore photographed recently and included in the Hitchin Triangle Design Statement Draft Consultation Document issued by the Triangle Residents Association in May 2009.

at 32 Walsworth Road which produces delicious food and charming service at an incredibly reasonable price.

The Radcliffe Arms restoration has smartened up that corner of the area very satisfactorily but has yet to establish itself as a Triangle meeting place. Sadly Cherry's hardware store in Nightingale Road has closed and although it appears to have turned into a house there remains in the front room rather more ironmongery than can realistically be used by any one family and limited opportunities exist for making purchases although the stock is not as wide as it was and you can no longer buy a light bulb and have it taken out of its packet and tested first. England may no longer be a nation of shopkeepers but the Cherrys seem to be a family of unstoppable ironmongers. You can't get tattooed by Ginger at 32 Walsworth Road any more but you can buy paraphernalia for making cards and join in craft groups.

And the scents of the Triangle! Incense drifts faintly from Holy Saviour on a Sunday morning and daily from about 6.00 p.m. the air is fragrant with Asian spices, oils and garlic wherever you wander, mingling with pizza and even regular English cooking wafting from the pubs which seem to keep going in spite of the vast numbers of closures about other parts of the land.

We miss the cheerful greetings of the Sikh Gurdwara particularly their magnificent Vaisakhi parade which set out annually from Radcliffe Road to wend its way through the town and the wild firework display that used to happen at the end of our garden but the transformation of the Gurdwara into the attractive Gainsford Court flats and cottages renews flagging confidence in at least one architect's sensibilities.

We are lucky enough to have at the heart of our area the Triangle Residents' Association beating quietly away giving a focus for friendly meeting and an opportunity to express concerns and attempt to safeguard treasured aspects or simply to organise a seaside coach trip or a fund raising curry evening. The late Di Shepherd was a staunch supporter of the Triangle Residents' Association and those of us involved with her caring, scribing and dog walking were honoured to be there through a sad yet remarkably brave time. (Her poem which ends this book, expresses more memorably life in the Triangle.)

In Ransoms Rec dog walkers meet, children and young people play and tucked away in one corner is the Triangle Community Garden with its willow maze, wild life pond and mosaic. I have left Vicky to tell you about its inception and how it works: a green lung carrying its own brand of nourishment to the heart."
(Vicky's contribution is to be found in the piece on Ransom's Recreation Ground in the Nightingale Road chapter)

Triangle Residents Association

Susan Dye, one of the "prime movers" in the Residents' Association wrote in October 2009:

"The Triangle Residents Association was established in 2000 as a neighbourhood project of the North Herts District Council Housing Department, led by Geoff Collins, a tenant participation officer. The initial focus was on council tenants' needs in Dacre and Radcliffe Roads, where some residents had concerns about council-owned temporary accommodation. Public meetings were held in Holy Saviour Church Hall. Geoff chaired the meetings and worked hard to get many and various council departments (County and District) to work together on problems such as drug dealing from "squatted" properties, burnt out cars on the 'in between lands' and joyriding at night in McDonalds car park. From the outset the police and local councillors Judi Billing, Martin Stears-Handscomb and David Billing were actively involved.

'What people don't realise is that this is our home and we want it to be the best it possibly can be'. This is a quote from the community survey conducted by the Triangle Residents Association (TRA) in 2003. Since then this active community group has been busy working with the District and County Council, Police and other authorities to make this lively and diverse part of Hitchin better for the people who live and work here.

The Triangle lies at the geographical centre of Hitchin and covers areas on and between Walsworth, Nightingale, Verulam, Kings, Alexandra, Dacre, Radcliffe, St Annes and Trevor Roads, Florence Street and Midland Cottages. The Association leaflets over 800 households four times a year to advertise its public meetings where residents raise issues with local councillors and other officials. In response to priorities revealed in the community survey, the group has successfully campaigned for traffic calming, a pedestrian refuge on Verulam Road and a safe crossing at the Recreation Ground entrance on the busy Nightingale Road, improvements to street lighting and extra street trees. The Association has also alerted residents to major planning applications in the area and gathered views and represented these to the council. For example, people were opposed to McDonalds opening till 1am and whilst not opposing high density housing, felt strongly that this should be in keeping with the local Victorian architecture. The Association also encouraged Val Taplin to establish the Triangle History Group responsible for the idea of this publication.

The happy, smiling faces of Triangle residents on their 2004 outing to Southwold in Suffolk.
(Bill Bowker)

In late 2001 Simon Young (a transport officer at NHDC) encouraged the Association to support a bid for government funding for a Home Zone in the Triangle, to 'redesign the streets for people' with slower traffic, street planting, seating and play equipment. The bid was unsuccessful, but the publicity it generated attracted a new committee member, Susan Dye, who was at that time working for a sustainable transport charity Transport 2000 and living in Walsworth Road. Her partner Ashley Walker had graphics skills and so the TRA newsletters started.

Being next to the railway station, car parking has been a continuing bugbear. Very few houses have driveways and in recent years increasing numbers of commuters would park in the streets. This caused real distress to vulnerable residents with mobility problems, those who needed regular carers to visit, parents with small children and shopping to handle. It was also difficult for visitors to the local shops and offices to park for short periods. Not all residents supported the idea of a permit scheme, but most saw that if a scheme were to be introduced in one area, it would push problems into the neighbouring streets. After five years working on this controversial issue, a sensitively designed parking scheme finally won enough support for a permit scheme to be introduced in February 2009 and most people agree that day to day conditions for residents with cars have improved as a result.

The TRA has a social side as well. For two years running the Association has taken a coach to the seaside and has also held a successful curry night, a family fun-day and even won a prize in the famous Hitchin Christmas Tree Festival held at Holy Saviour Church.

At the time of writing, the major TRA project is to complete a planning 'Design Statement' to guide future planning applications for the area. (The Design Statement has since been completed) There is also ongoing support for anti-crime initiatives with the 'Online Watch Line' (OWL) Neighbourhood Watch scheme. (This is now up and running). Plenty of other opportunities for new projects remain. One longstanding idea, still at the concept stage, is to adopt the area between Radcliffe and Dacre Roads. There is also a proposal to raise funds to restore the railings at the entrance to Ransoms Recreation Ground. (This has probably been shelved for the time being).

In community activism you have to have staying power and patience to see things change. The TRA has been tireless in speaking up for the Triangle and welcomes residents who come and speak their minds in meetings. This 'fire in the belly' is what creates the energy

One of the chimney pots in the Cloisters in Radcliffe Road, where Diane spent her last days

to get things changed. People get involved for different reasons. I was interested in better conditions for walking and cycling. So of course I am delighted we got the new pedestrian crossings. But along the way I discovered a wonderful group of people living on my doorstep. I would recommend anyone to get involved in a local community group. Together people can achieve far, far more than will ever be achieved by acting alone".

Richard Field has kindly allowed this poem written by his late wife to be reproduced in full. She spent the last months of her life in the Cloisters in Radcliffe Road and her poem sums up the atmosphere and the affection of the Triangle's residents for their piece of Hitchin.

Radcliffe Road has given me so much I would like to leave it with a blessing.

May your old people be honoured
May your children be nurtured
May the cats grow sleek on your windowsills
May the squirrels recall their winter hoards
May the frogs spawn in your ponds
May your waterbutts overflow
May your trees flourish and choirs of birds
Sing hallelujah every dawning
May the youths who lurk in dark alleys throw away their fixings
And go down to Mollys
For a pint of Guinness and the good craic
May your Church and Temple unite in friendship
And praising the God of generosity and the open heart
May news of your warmth roll across Ransoms Rec to the Community Garden
Yeah even unto the Kingdom Hall
And when the new folk move into Lavender Fields
May they say to themselves
Let's try and create a neighbourhood like the one in Radcliffe Road.

Diane Shepherd 30.3.2006

Cloisters footscraper

Sources

Printed Sources

Alleyne's School(Stevenage) Old Boys' Association, 1989 — An Innings Well Played — The Story of Alleyne's School, Stevenage 1558 – 1989

Armitage, E N — The Quaker Poets of Great Britain and Ireland. Andrews, 1896

Beds. & Herts. Pictorial (Hospital Supplement) — 16th July, 1929

Campion, V — Pioneering Women. *Hitchin Historical Society, 2008*

Cannon, Reg — The first hundred years (of Holy Saviour Church). *Centenary Year booklet printed by S.G.* Street & Co Ltd, Baldock, 1965

Cockman, F. G. — The Railways of Hertfordshire. *Hertfordshire Publications, 2nd ed, 1983*

Dargert, Leslie. — A walk around Hitchin in words and pictures. *GPR Printing, 1993*

Douglas, P. & Humphries, P. — Discovering Hitchin. *Egon Publishers Ltd, 1995*

Douglas, P. & Humphries, P. — The Hitchin Cabmen's Shelter. *Hitchin Historical Society, 1998*

Douglas, P. & Humphries, P. (eds). — The House that Bartlett Built. *Hitchin Historical Society, 1996*

Fitzpatrick, Sue and West, Barry. — Street names of Hitchin and their origins. *Book I.* The town centre. Egon Publishers, 1997

Fleck, A. — Exploring Hitchin. *Hitchin Historical Society, 2006. (CD ROM)*

Foster, A.M. — Market Town: Hitchin in the nineteenth century. *Hitchin Historical Society, 1987*

Foster, A.M. — The sad tale of the Morris Guy Fire Engine — Hitchin History leaflet, No.3. *Hitchin Historical Society, June 1980*

Gadd, Pat. — Fifty years of change in Hitchin. *1980*

Gadd, P. — Hitchin Inns (an unpublished manuscript)

Gadd, P. & Pigram, R. — Hitchin Inns and Incidents. *Pat Gadd, 1978*

Gordon, D.I. — Regional history of the railways of Great Britain, Vol.5. *David & Charles, 1990*

Hankin, Peter A. — A History of Walsworth Road Baptist Church Hitchin Hertfordshire 1867-1992

Hawkes, Valerie, — comp Offley monumental inscriptions. *Hertfordshire Family & Population History Society, 1985*

Hine, Reginald. — Obituary of Ralph Erskine Sanders. *Herts & Cambs Reporter, September 1st 1933*

Hitchin Girls' Grammar School magazine 1917

Hitchin Journal, — 2003, 2007

Howard, P — Take the train from Hitchin. *Hitchin Historical Society, 2006*

Howlett, D — Hitchin and the GNER 1850-2000. *Hitchin Historical Society, 2006*

Howlett, Bridget — Survey of the Royal Manor of Hitchin 1676. *(Herts Record Society, Vol. 16), 2000*

Jolliffe, G. & Jones, A— Hertfordshire Inns and Public Houses: an historical gazetteer. *Hertfordshire Publications, 1995*

Lucas, E.S. — A Selection of Poems. *Headley Bros.,* 1890

Old Hitchin: — Portrait of an English Market Town from the Cameras of T.B.Latchmore and others. *Commentary by Alan Fleck & Helen Poole, Phillimore, 1999*

Poole, H. — "Here for the Beer!" a Gazetteer of The Brewers of Hertfordshire. *Watford Museum, 1984*

Railway Magazine, — Vol 51, No 306, December 1922

Shaw, D.H. — The History of St Michael's and the Catholic Parish of Hitchin. *The Old Michaelean Association, 1975.*

Shields, Pamela — Hertfordshire Secrets and Spies. *Amberley 2009*

Spencer, Sylvia — Convent memories. *The Book Guild, 1997*

Tales of Tilehouse Street — cine film script, quoting lecture by Reginald Hine, 1941

Victoria History of the Counties of England: — County of Hertfordshire, Vol.3. *Dawsons for the University of London Institute of Historical research, 1971 reprint of original edition 1912*

West, Barry — Street names of Hitchin and their origins Book II Eastern Hitchin. *Egon Publishers, 1998*

Hitchin Museum
Hitchin Charities Records 1836.
Hitchin Fire brigade Records, 1867-1911, Vols 1-7 and Vol.11, February 8th 1913
Loftus Barham and Lawson Thompson Scrapbooks
Map Collection
Newspaper Archive – Hertfordshire Express, 1865-1933
Regency Directory of Hitchin and District 1968/9

Hitchin Library
Census Records 1841-1901
Handbook to Hitchin 1899
Hitchin Directories, 1931-1960
Kelly's Directories, 1906 – 1937
Map collection - 1844, 1852, 1881, 1898
Newspapers   Comet 1999, 2009
        Hertfordshire Countryside 1984
        Hertfordshire on Sunday, 2000

Monthly Advertiser, 1865
North Herts Gazette, 1975
Trade Directories

Hertfordshire Archives and Local Studies
Local directories, photographs, deposited church documents
and on-line resources

Holy Saviour Church Documents
Early accounts, sketches & plans of church, school, orphanage &
almshouses buildings.
Church magazines
Scrapbooks
Church registers
Royal Commission on Ecclesiastical Discipline, Vol.I

Her Majesty's Courts Service. York Probate Sub-Registry

Religious Society of Friends Hitchin Meeting.
List of Interments in Burial Ground

Bedfordshire County Council Archives

Internet sources
www.ancestry.co.uk
www.salvationarmy.org/history
www.hertsdirect.org/hals
www.nationalarchives.gov.uk/records/catalogues-and-online-records.htm
www.architecture.com/LibraryDrawingsandPhotographs/Home.aspx

Index

Hitchin Historical Society

The Society aims to increase and spread knowledge of the history of Hitchin, and is a registered charity. We hold regular meetings on the fourth Thursday of most months and arrange visits to local buildings and institutions, many of which are not normally open to the general public. We also organize trips to places of historical interest further afield. Members receive a regular newsletter and magazine, the Hitchin Journal. The Society also produces high-quality publications on the history of the town based on research into the origins and development of buildings, organizations, crafts, trades and other aspects of historical interest.